THE MEMORY
OF
MANKIND

The Story of Libraries
Since the Dawn of History

Don Heinrich Tolzmann,
Alfred Hessel and Reuben Peiss

Heritage Books
2025

HERITAGE BOOKS

AN IMPRINT OF HERITAGE BOOKS, INC.

Books, CDs, and more—Worldwide

For our listing of thousands of titles see our website
at
www.HeritageBooks.com

A Facsimile Reprint
Published 2025 by
HERITAGE BOOKS, INC.
Publishing Division
5810 Ruatan Street
Berwyn Heights, MD 20740

Library of Congress Cataloging-in-Publication Data
Tolzmann, Don Heinrich, 1945–
    The memory of mankind: the story of libraries since the dawn of history / Don
Heinrich Tolzmann, Alfred Hessel, and Reuben Peiss
    p. cm.
    Rev. and updated ed. of A history of libraries by Alfed Hessel, which was
translated, with supplementary material added, by Reuben Peiss and published in 1950.
    Includes bibliographical references and index.
    ISBN: 1-58456-049-5
    1. Libraries—History. I Hessel, Alfred, 1877–1939. II. Peiss, Reuben, 1912–1952.
III. Hessel, Alfred, 1877–1939. Geschichte der bibliotheken. English. IV. Title.

Z721 .H582 2001
027'.009—dc21

International Standard Book Number
Paperbound: 978-0-7884-5092-1

TABLE OF CONTENTS

ACKNOWLEDGMENTS

In 1925, Alfred Hessel, University of Göttingen, published a general history of libraries, *Geschichte der Bibliotheken: Ein Überblick von ihren Anfängen bis zur Gegenwart* which was especially valued as it provided as concise introduction to the topic.[1] Moreover, it placed libraries within the broader historical context of the times in which they emerged, thereby linking them to the social, cultural, and political life of world history. In 1950, Reuben Peiss, University of California-Berkeley, published a translated edition of the history with updates to mid-century.[2] This made Hessel's work more widely accessible in the U.S. However, since that time, more than half a century has elapsed, and there have been numerous developments in the world of libraries with the advent of the information age. It, therefore, seemed appropriate to bring out a revised and expanded edition of this work. In editing it, the text has been thoroughly reviewed, and revisions made where necessary, so that it has been brought up-to-date. Also, a selective bibliography of basic sources has been added. Then as now, the purpose of the work is to provide an introductory survey of the historical development of libraries from their earliest beginnings.

My motivation for bringing out a new edition of this work came about as a result of teaching "Library and Book History" for the University of Kentucky School of Library and Information Science. As a graduate of the School, who had studied the history of books, printing and publishing with Robert E. Cazden, and library history with Michael H. Harris, the opportunity of teaching, what I had once studied with them, was obviously of great interest, and I am clearly indebted to both of them. Hence, a word of gratitude is in order on the occasion of the publication of this work. Special thanks to Dorothy Young, Department of Germanic Languages and Literatures, for the preparation of the manuscript. Thanks also to Kevin Grace, Archives and Rare Books Department, University of Cincinnati, for copies of the historic postcards of libraries from his private collection. Finally, thanks to Konstantinos Staikos for the loan of many of his illustrations, and John Lewis von Hoelle, Publishing Director of the Oak Knoll Press, for all that he has done to make this work possible.

Don Heinrich Tolzmann
University of Cincinnati

PREFACE

The institution known as the library is almost as old as recorded history. Buried in the drifting sands of ancient Mesopotamia, archeologists have excavated dozens of temple and palace libraries filled with tens-of-thousands of cuneiform-inscribed clay tablets. It seems as soon as man invented the wondrous art of writing he wanted to preserve and protect his ingenious handiwork. The oldest of these archives dates from circa 3000 B.C.E.

The basic function of the library has changed little in the past five millennia. They still serve to collect and preserve the memories of man's endeavor. The history of the library is also the celebration of the immortality of the written word. Libraries make available to all, the thoughts of famous philosophers, pharaohs and prophets. They also preserve the precious wisdom of countless scholars, poets and teachers. They serve us by sharing the experiences of remarkable people who have made us proud to be human; and made us wiser by recording the dark deeds of madmen—least we forget.

As an institution, libraries have survived the fall of empires and the follies of man and nature. And in doing so, they have bequeathed to us a unique legacy of man's literary achievement unsurpassed.

In *The Memory of Mankind,* librarian and scholar Don Heinrich Tolzmann updates and expands the original 1925 German-language classic of Alfred Hessel and its English translation by Reuben Peiss. His excellent research and well-written text adds an array of new insight and information to the fascinating history of this remarkable institution.

Whether from ideas pressed into clay tablets, printed on paper, or encrypted in binary code, Tolzmann believes the libraries of the future will continue to be the depositories and guardians of man's knowledge for millennia to come—just as they have for the past 5,000 years.

J. Lewis von Hoelle

As the memory data banks of humankind, libraries collect and make accessible the historical record. Indeed, pre-historic time is distinguished from the dawn of history by absence of written records for the former. History begins with historical materials, and the assemblage of them into collections for use marks the beginnings of library history. Since writing is thought to have begun around 3,000 B.C., the beginnings of library history began sometime thereafter in antiquity.

The word "library" comes from the Latin word *liber*, which means book. but libraries, of course preceded books as we know them today. Indeed, the earliest libraries housed collections consisting of clay tablets, papyrus, and scrolls. Hence, the term library may be defined as a collection of graphic informational materials, assembled for a particular purpose or reason, which are then organized and made accessible for use. The basic function of a library, therefore, is to collect, preserve, organize, and make such materials available.

Let Goethe's maxim be emphasized once more: libraries are the memory of mankind. How they developed and came to be what they are today, and where they are headed, is the focal point of this work.

DHT

For more than three thousand years, cuneiform tablets made it possible for ancient librarians to collect and preserve the history, sciences, languages, culture, and religion of their people. These remarkable inscribed clay tablets became an early part of "the memory of mankind."

The Memory of Mankind

Chapter I. The Ancient World

Libraries have served as the memory of mankind by preserving the records of civilization since the dawn of history. Indeed, the library is one of the oldest institutions in the history of civilization, but it is much more than that. The library may very well be viewed as one of the pillars of civilization, without which a given culture or society cannot be imagined. History begins with the written record; however there has to be more than a scattered number of written records for there to be a library and/or a civilization. Works have to be preserved, collected, and organized for study, research, and reflection. When this was accomplished, the institution that came to be called "the library" was born. This new institution became a foundational element in the emergence and development of a civilization and culture.

What is a civilization? According to the dictionary, it is the sum qualities of a particular civilized society. What is "civilized" in this context? Referring to the dictionary again, we find that to civilize is "to endow with law, order, and the conditions favorable to the arts and sciences." How can this scheme of things be conceived of without the institution of the library? Library history, hence, goes hand in hand with the history of civilization, and the two are inextricably woven together in one fabric.

However, it may be said that neither stands alone, although it is the institution of the library that is rarely illuminated in history. Nevertheless, like the air we breath, the water we drink, it is essential to the life of all civilizations from the beginnings of time to the present.

Another striking feature to take into consideration in setting out to explore the institution that has saved the memory of mankind is the remarkable degree to which the basic concept and principles of libraries, which were created in antiquity, have stood the test of time, and, indeed so much so, that they are taken for granted. The Old Testament prophet Isaiah opined that there was nothing new under the sun, and this truism applies to libraries as well. Yes, there have been, and will be, a never-ending stream of technological innovations, but they appear to be mere variations on the basic themes defined in antiquity as to the goals, purposes, and principles relating to the institution of the library.

Thus the significance of library history relates directly to the origins of the history of civilization and culture, and understanding its role in this context contributes not only to an awareness of one of the oldest institutions in existence, but the one that has preserved and transmitted the wisdom and knowledge of the ages.

Archeologists have discovered some of the earliest examples of libraries among the ruins of the most ancient cities of the Tigris Euphrates valleys. Excavations have revealed many *"Houses of Tablets"* attached to excavated temples and royal palaces. Within these libraries of clay tablets were found the literary, political, scientific, and religious wisdom of their age. In the libraries of the Sumerian city of Uruk, the earliest known inscripted tablets were dated before 3000 B.C.E. At Sumerian Ur (circa 2600 B.C.E.) thousands of cuneiform inscribed tablets were found revealing a rich tradition in epic literature as well as texts on mathematics, medicine, and the oldest versions of the

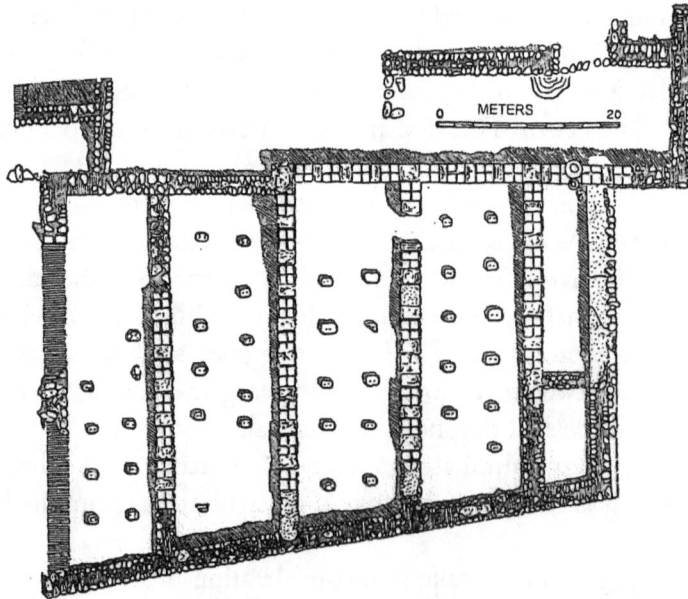

Figure 1: Floor plan of the royal library in the Hittite capital of Boghazköy. In its seven rooms were found buried thousands of clay tablets in several languages.

Creation and Deluge myths. In the ancient Syrian city of Ebla (circa 2300 B.C.E.) a complete royal library was discovered still organized in its original classifications. Archeologists at Sumerian Sippar and the Hittite capital of Boghazkoy have also recovered entire libraries with their wealth of records intact. Excavations in the ancient mounds of Mari, Nippur, Nuzi, and dozens of other sites have revealed still more libraries with a few hundred tablets to more than 40,000.

To date, over 600,000 inscribed tablets in more than 250 sites have been recovered and archaeologists suggest these represent only a small portion of the vast qualities believed still buried in the sands and dusty mounds of the Near East. When these tablets are fully translated and understood we will have an understanding of our origins as never before.

Perhaps one of the greatest of the ancient libraries was found during the excavations of the Assyrian capital at Nineveh in the mid-nineteenth century. This incredible depository held over 30,000 tablets and due to the almost indestructible nature of the material, the library survives to this day relatively intact at the British Museum and Philadelphia's University Museum. This literary wonder of the ancient world began as a standard royal archive containing the king's decrees, inventories, and correspondence with his far-flung officials. That is, until Assurbanipal (669–633 B.C.E.) became King of Assyria and ruler of Egypt and Babylonia; an empire of the then-known civilized world.

Assurbanipal's goal was to collect every known work related to the social, cultural, and religious heritage of his empire. He sent agents to libraries throughout the empire to collect or copy such works. At Nineveh he established a scriptorium where new editions of these works could be produced and annotated. The library itself was divided into two parts: materials pertaining to correspondence, governmental records, and business accounts were in one section, and literary, historical, religious, scientific, and scholarly works were kept in the other part. Here, historical chronologies could be found, as well as lists of high ranking officials. It also contained several editions of *The Epic of Gilgamesh,* and the verse Creation Epic, which was more than several thousand lines in length.

Assurbanipal's library held a wealth of materials dealing with astrology, medicine, and religion, as well as a great deal of physiological information about humans and animals. In short, the library functioned as an encyclopedia of human knowledge about humankind and the universe. Royal scribes were commissioned by the king to manage and maintain the library at Nineveh. They not only copied ancient texts, they also added explanatory notes, thus providing the earliest editions of ancient works. Moreover, some of them were authors of their own works as well. Therefore, these early

Figure 2: Assurbanipal (669–633 B.C.E.), warrior, king, and scholar.

librarians were authors and scholars, as well as scribes. And in their care was the memory of mankind for 3,000 years.

After the Royal Library of Nineveh, the founding of the Library of Alexandria may be called the second greatest accomplishment in the library history of ancient times.[1] The planning of this library is ascribed to Ptolemy Soter (d. ca. 283 B.C.), the first of the Diadochian dynasty in Egypt, and the execution of the plan to his son, Ptolemy Philadelphus. Since they proposed nothing less than collecting the whole of Greek literature, these rulers must have had to make available very large funds. Furthermore, they did not balk at various unscrupulous methods: for example, they confiscated the book cargoes of ships anchoring in the harbor of Alexandria, and (the story goes) having borrowed from Athens the works of the three great tragedians, they returned not the official text which had been borrowed but only a copy of it. The number of papyrus rolls finally assembled was reckoned to be several hundred thousand—a prodigious total, even when one considers that in it were included many duplicates and that, moreover, a single literary work as a rule covered several rolls. The library was in two divisions, the large one within the royal palace in the Brucheum section of the city, and the small one in the Temple of Serapis. After the former was destroyed in 47 B.C. during Caesar's campaign in Alexandria, the Serapeum became the real book center of the city.

There were undeniably remarkable resemblances between the libraries of Nineveh and Alexandria. Both were institutions of a universal character brought into being by reigning princes. It is also proper to point out that in more than one respect the inner organization of the Hellenistic library calls to mind the Assyrian library, and that there are even many similarities in the treatment of the individual literary work in both places despite the difference in writing material (clay tablets at Nineveh, papyrus rolls at Alexandria).

An investigation into library conditions in Greece gives promise of better results; indeed, our word for the institution points to Greek origin.[3] Libraries emerged in early classical times. As early as the 6th century B.C., public libraries were established by Polycrates of Samos and Pisistratus of Athens. The latter, established in 560 B.C., was unfortunately destroyed in 480 B.C., when Athens was sacked by Xerxes, who took the collection to Persia, from whence it eventually returned to Athens in the 3rd century B.C. after Seleucus I Nicator's conquest of Persia. There was, moreover, a well-developed book trade in the time of Pericles, and at the onset of the fourth century B.C. it became more frequent for scholars or literary men to collect libraries of their own. For example, a remark in one of Aristophanes' comedies makes it probable that Euripides did so.[4] The full development of the Greek library began, then, in the very decades which embraced the activity of those two intellectual giants, Plato and Aristotle.

The Academy and the Peripatetic school can claim the glory of having created "not only the learning of Greece but of classical antiquity as a whole.": Here there developed for the first time "a large-scale organization of cooperative work" under the leadership of a single individual. Plato undertook a methodical investigation into the fields of mathematics and natural science. Aristotle strove, insofar as possible, to collect completely and establish on a sound footing the facts in all the branches of knowledge, and he became the father of the disciplines of philological criticism and literary history. The work of both these men unquestionably presupposes the existence of a considerable library. With regard to Plato we have no definite report of such a library; of Aristotle, on the contrary, we hear that he collected manuscripts systematically, and we know also of the vicissitudes suffered by the library which he left behind.

Aristotle's pupil, Alexander the Great, opened a new period of ancient history through his campaigns. Greek culture broadened its scope, becoming a world civiliza-

Figure 3: Aristotle, from a manuscript of his Historia naturalis, *Rome 1457 (Cod. vindob. phil. gr. 64).*

tion. An international class of educated men came into being. In Hellenistic culture scholarship and erudition became important factors of intellectual life. The seed sown by Aristotle now bore rich fruit, yet there was at the same time a change in the direction of scholarly endeavor. The unifying bond with which the master had connected the special field of knowledge became more and more relaxed. These individual fields of knowledge became independent; investigations were confined to limited subject matter; and not infrequently the accumulation of knowledge handed down by preceding generations took the place of creative work. Furthermore, the outer form of intellectual cooperation also changed. The free school of philosophers turned into a monarchical organization. For Hellensim adopted as its own form of state the kingdom of the Diadochi, and these princes considered it their task to foster and to propagate Greek culture.

Alexander himself died too early to raise the large-scale organization of scientific studies in the spirit of the Stagirite to the status of a governmental program. This was accomplished by the first Ptolemy, who found a spiritual adviser in the Peripatetic, Demetrius of Phalerum. The Museum was founded on the Athenian model, and the most outstanding scholars of the time were called to the Egyptian court, so that Alexandria swiftly developed into the center of Hellenistic learning. The library constituted the most important working unit of the Museum. A systematic study of Greek literature was undertaken, authoritative texts put together by means of philological and historical criticism, problems of authorship and authenticity investigated, and the extent and division of literary works determined. At the same time the Alexandrian school had an epoch-making effect upon the whole field of the book arts, in that it produced standard copies of individual authors and of the different forms of literature. These were reproduced by a large number of copyists, and copies were then placed on sale. Thus it was to the Museum and its library that Alexandria owed its monopoly on the book trade, which it maintained up to the time of Caesar.

From what we have already said it is easy to understand that administration of the Alexandrian collections was entrusted only to coryphaei of learning, especially since they had, at the same time, to occupy the exalted position of royal tutor. The first of these was the great grammarian, Zenodotus of Ephesus (d. ca. 260 B.C.). He began the arrangement of the book stock and started the editing of Greek literature with his edition of Homer. Of his successors we must mention Eratosthenes, a universal mind encompassing the arts and sciences, known above all as the founder of chronology and of mathematical geography, and Aristophanes of Byzantium, whose most important contribution is to be found in the field of lexicography. Callimachus of Cyrene occupied a special place in this list. Some do not consider him a member of the library staff

Figure 4: Alexander the Great rescuing the classics by Homer. By M. Raimondi.

at all; others consider him some kind of subordinate official. The scholarly reputation of Callimachus rests upon his *Pinakes*, which he produced about the middle of the third century B.C., probably by availing himself of previous foreign work and the help of disciples. These comprised catalogues of the manuscripts in the library, separated prose writers from poets, and broke up both divisions into subject groups. Within each of these groups the authors were arranged alphabetically and each one provided with a biographical notice and a list of his writings. Finally, the individual work was described as to title, first words, and number of lines. These *Pinakes* for a long time enjoyed a canonical reputation and formed the basis of all later bibliographies of antiquity.

Concerning the spatial arrangement of the library of Alexandria we know nothing definite. This makes even more valuable, therefore, the results obtained by the German excavations at Pergamum at the end of the 19th century. The library there was the work of the Attali: Eumenes II (197–158 B.C.) is considered its founder. Near the temple of Athena Polias an open court with a two-storied portico with four adjoining rooms was uncovered. In the largest was found the great statue of Athena and also pedestal inscriptions referring to well-known writers of Asia Minor, among them one in verse on

Homer. Here we have the typical layout of the ancient library: the stoa serving as a study, the entrance hall adorned with statues, and the remaining chambers given over to book storage—the whole closely adjoining a temple.[5]

One very slight information has come down to us concerning the founding of libraries by others of the Diadochi, for example the libraries of the Seleucids, which were certainly very important. On the whole, the sources for that period are so meager that the very important process of development which the Hellenistic library had

Figure 5: The Great Library of Alexandria. By O. von Corven

then to undergo has remained almost totally unobserved. From all appearances the manuscript collection at Alexandria represented originally only a research tool for a limited group of scholars. Gradually the number of users must have become larger and larger. Thus the library at the Athenian academy located within the Ptolemeum may already have taken on more the appearance of a modern university library. It represented another important step forward when to those interested in scholarship was added the broad circle of educated men in general. Thereby the library for the first time acquired a truly public character and no longer confined itself to serving as a place for work, but existed now, to use Vitruvius's phrase, "for the enjoyment of all" (*ad communem delectationem*). This type, too, we may assume, the Hellenistic period had already worked out; for this it was which the civilization of the eastern Mediterranean handed over to the western Mediterranean at the end of the first century B.C.

"Conquered Greece subdued her savage conqueror,"[6] says the ancient poet. Modern scholarship sees in the culture of the Roman Empire only a continuation and further development of Hellenistic culture.

From the middle of the second century B.C. Roman generals began to bring home Greek libraries along with other booty. The first to do this was Aemilius Paulus, and in the next century Sulla and Lucullus followed his example. Toward the end of the

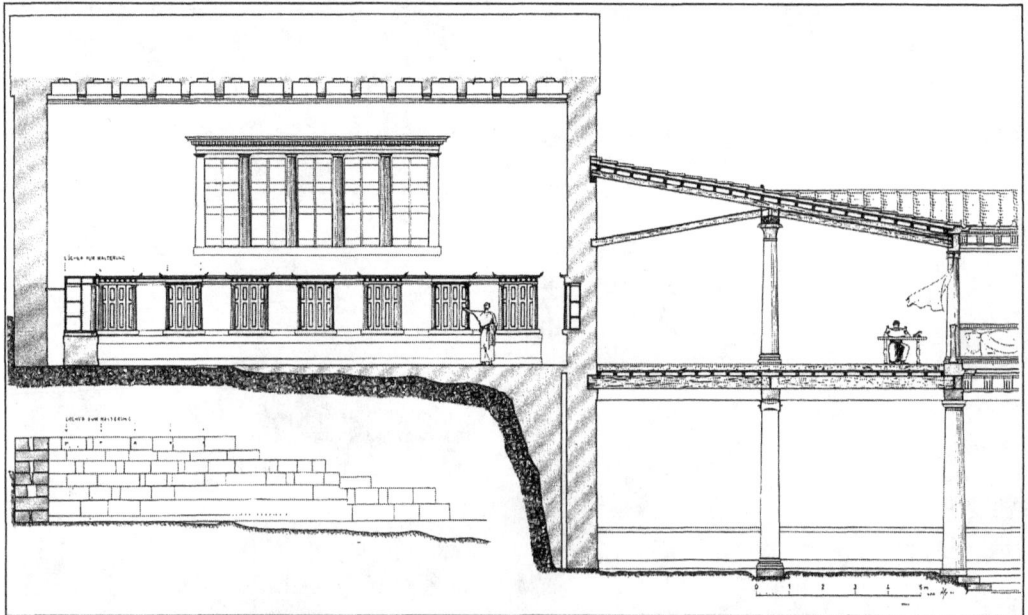

Figure 6: Reconstruction drawing of the Royal Library at Pergamum. By W. Hoepfner.

Figure 7: Reconstruction of a cabinet, Royal Library at Pergamum. By W. Hoepfner.

Figure 8: Part of the central facade of Hadrian's Library in Athens. By J. Stuart and N. Revett.

first century B.C. love of books spread among the Roman aristocracy. Cicero valued his collection very highly and saw in it the heart of his home. His friend Atticus was Rome's first large publisher and dared even to compete with the Alexandrian book trade. He was himself well-educated and he employed a staff of collaborators thoroughly trained in philology, among them Varro, who even wrote a treatise entitled *De Bibliothecis.*[7]

Caesar was eager to avail himself of Varro's help so that by founding a state library he might, as Mommsen says, "bind together world domination and world literature." Culturally Caesar's endeavors show themselves clearly patterned after Hellenistic models. There is a good deal of evidence that he harbored the intention of transplanting the Alexandrian Library to the Tiber. But not until after his death was the first public library established in Rome in the *Atrium Libertatis.* It was one of Caesar's intimate friends, Asinius Pollio, who in this way "was the first to make men's talents public property."[8] Augustus followed suit by establishing two collections—one on the Palatine at the temple of Apollo, the other in the *Porticus Octaviae.* At the opening of the fourth century A.D. the public libraries in the capital city numbered twenty-eight. Only a few of them can be identified. Still, we are justified in assuming that collections were hardly wanting at the great forums and baths. The most important was the *Bibliotheca Ulpia* near the Column of Trajan.[9] Like the others, it was divided into a Greek and a Latin division, and it served also as the archive for important state documents. Heading these libraries at first were distinguished scholars with the rank of *procurator.* Later there developed a distinction between the administrative officials proper and the scholarly directors. Under them served slaves or freedmen so numerous as to require their own physician.

The cities of Italy and the provinces endeavored to follow the example of Rome. Neither the casual references in literary remains nor the results of excavations undertaken in various places permit even an approximate estimate of the number of public libraries in the expanse of the Empire. One gets the impression that probably the majority of the larger provincial cities with intellectual interests had their libraries.[10] Occasionally they were indebted for their erection to the munificence of an emperor—thus the Greek-loving Hadrian presented to Athens a magnificent library, the ruins of which one can still marvel at today—but mostly they were due to the liberality of private citizens. These people looked after their own needs no less earnestly, for bibliophilic inclinations were in fashion in the time of the Roman Empire. No aristocratic city palace, no grand villa found it seemly to fail to have its book collection. Hence Seneca's jibe: "Nowadays a library is considered a necessary ornament with which to adorn a house along with hot and cold baths";[11] and, in another place: "What is the

Figure 9: Reconstruction, Cicero in his library. 18th century engraving.

use of innumerable books and libraries if in a lifetime the master hardly reads the titles?"[12] There were private libraries with 30,000 and even 60,000 rolls. the master of the house either kept educated slaves for their production or he met his needs with the help of the very highly developed book trade. Among the educated, Greek authors were much preferred. Our most reliable information concerning the contents of such a library comes from the famous discovery of book rolls at Herculaneum, which is today one of the treasures of the museum at Naples.

In general the physical arrangement of Roman libraries followed the principles already familiar to us from Pergamum, though naturally this did not preclude individual differences. Thus the latest excavations at Ephesus have brought to light a book-room without a portico but having instead a facade with ornamental columns and an outside staircase.[13] Vitruvius urged that the rooms face the East to take advantage of the morning light, but in practice his requirements were not always fulfilled. In order specially to protect the papyrus rolls from dampness an outer wall was frequently built around the inner wall, so that a narrow passage ran between the two. For the rest, so far as stone work, architectural style, and artistic decoration are concerned, libraries resembled the other monumental structures of the age. Very likely there was always a statue of some deity which was placed usually in a recess of the great hall. Accompanying it were busts and medallions of scholars and writers "whose immortal souls speak in these very places" (*immortales animae in locis iisdem loquuntur*). A good deal of ornamentation was in evidence, but in order to spare the eyes, gold was avoided and a greenish marble selected for the floors. The book rolls, with tickets bearing their titles outward, lay in the pigeon-holes of the wooden presses. These were often symmetrically arranged and sunk into niches in the walls. When necessary there were several such rows, one above the other. The top rows were then reached by means of galleries, which rested on columns. We can say nothing exact about leading practices in the arrangement of the book stock, since only quite scanty fragments of catalogues have been preserved. Some of the public libraries circulated their books. Their administration was frequently in the hands of priests when, as very commonly occurred, they were connected with a temple.

The history of Graeco-Roman libraries covers a period of about 600 years. It could point to achievements which the Christian West was able to match only after a period of development three times as long. This superiority of the ancient libraries was indeed well known to succeeding generations. Our exposition will show in how many ways the creations of antiquity hovered before the eyes of much later library reformers as ideals.

SCHEMA VOLUMINUM, IN BIBLIOTHECAM ORDINE OLIM DIGESTORUM,
Noviomagi in loco Castrorum Constantini M. ho:
diedum in lapide reperto excisum .

Figure 10: Engraving made from a lost Roman relief at Neumagen on the Moselle.

Chapter II. The Middle Ages To Charlemagne

Historians nowadays avoid drawing a distinct line of demarcation between the ancient world and the Middle Ages; instead they suggest a period of transition lasting a good five hundred years. Accordingly no exact span of years can be specified in which the ancient library ceased to exist and the medieval library had its inception. Scholars must content themselves with identifying each of the main factors which determined the character of this new type of library and with following the course of its development.[1]

A signal characteristic of the ancient library is the papyrus roll, of the medieval library, the parchment codex. In the preceding chapter we became acquainted with papyrus as the writing material of

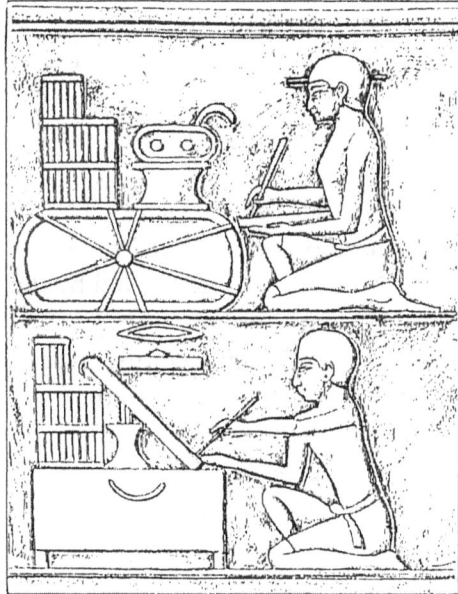

Figure 11: Egyptian scribe at work. Drawing from the tomb of Khunar by Faucher-Gudin.

ancient times. Even then, as a matter of fact, parchment was used for less important purposes, but artistic and literary evidence indicates that it first came into more general use in the third century A.D., and by the fifth century it had almost entirely supplanted papyrus. In this period, therefore, took place the transcription of most of the extant literature from one writing material to the other, a process whose importance for the textual criticism carried on in modern philology is well known. And now, corresponding to the substitution of parchment or papyrus, in these centuries the parchment codex with a stiff cover replaced the papyrus roll as the physical form of books. It is to be expected that the infiltration of the parchment codex brought with it certain changes in the internal structure of the library. Still, these could not have been of a revolutionary nature; at least a mosaic of the fifth century and a miniature of the sixth century show that the codices were kept in chests, just as the rolls had been formerly. If accommodating the new form of book demanded considerably more space than before, this disadvantage was in a measure compensated for by the fact that a single codex could contain the texts of a whole series of papyrus rolls.

Its real advantages—greater durability and ease of handling, the possibility of writing on both sides, and other features—decided the victory of the parchment codex over the papyrus roll. But we should also consider the simultaneous operation of non-material factors. Thus it seems to have been a time in which the new form of book was propagated by the religious power then coming to the fore, Christianity, while pagan culture, placed on the defensive, was clinging to the form which was on the way out. It was probably about the same time that the Christian library entered into competition with the pagan.

Figure 12: St. Augustine in his library. 15th century painting.

The fate of the pagan library was closely tied up with that of ancient culture. With that culture falling into decay, one school of rhetoricians after another shutting down, and the number of unlettered people rapidly increasing, desolation settled upon the places where formerly those interested in pagan science and literature used to foregather. In the fourth century Ammianus Marcellinus is already lamenting the "libraries closed forever like tombs" (*bybliothecae sepulchrorum ritu in perpetuum claustrae*).[2] Upon the heels of desolation came destruction. We have practically no trustworthy accounts of the dispersal of manuscripts and the tearing down of buildings. The

Alexandrian Library appears to have fallen prey to Christian fanaticism at the end of the fourth century A.D.; and it is said that the same Gregory the Great who preached the famous "funeral sermons" to a Rome oppressed by the Lombards caused the imperial book collections to be burned. This comes down, to be sure, as a much later tradition of the Middle Ages, yet it contains the kernel of truth latent in every legend.

In structure Christian libraries copied the pagan ones. As so many of the latter were located within temples, it was natural to bring the former within houses of worship and therewith to assure them of the protection of the Church. The books of the Bible (hence also designated *biblia sacra* or *divina*) everywhere formed the basis of the collection. To these were then added liturgical and exegetical writings, and from the time when Christian apologetics began to expand, the works of the theologians and their heathen opponents could no longer be missing. Finally, for studying and gaining proficiency in the language of the Church, be it Greek or Latin, the remaining profane literature was needed.

We have information about many a church library, especially in Africa, even before the reign of Diocletian. Many fell victim to his great persecution. But, from the time the church was raised by Constantine to the rank of a state institution, the disciplinary, organizational, and dogmatic duties of each bishop forced him at least to maintain a library of moderate compass. At the opening of the fifth century Paulinus of Nola even built at his episcopal seat a Christian reading room and provided it with the inscription: "Here he whose thoughts are on the laws of God may sit and ponder over holy books."[3]

Tertullian (ca. 200) was one of the first of the Church Fathers whose library we can picture today. Then we also have details of the widely renowned library of Caesarea in Palestine. The oldest part of its collection consisted of the manuscripts of Origen, which his pupil Pamphilus (d. 309) copied and industriously augmented. Approximately one hundred years later Jerome made use of them and was able to report that two bishops of Caesarea had transferred to parchment the papyrus rolls of Pamphilus. Jerome was himself an ardent book-collector. His contemporary, the great Augustine, also left valuable manuscripts to the Church at Hippo. These scholars' libraries divided naturally into three parts: two profane, divided by language, and one Christian. The Church Fathers no longer used profane literature in the classical way, for because of their faith they could never overcome a deep-rooted aversion to pagan literature. It served them much more simply as an expedient, a base upon which to build Christian knowledge.

The fifth and sixth centuries brought the political collapse of the Roman Empire and the founding of the German states in the western provinces. Most recent studies

Figure 13: Reconstruction of a library of Christian works.

have been right in trying to delimit the effect of these events upon the general development of culture, and, above all, in denying the theory of a general catastrophe. In contrast to former centuries there was a strongly increasing influx of Germanic peoples who found themselves up against a strange culture and language. As a consequence, the kind of education provided in ancient times became even less widespread among the laity and, correspondingly, the Church securely established its position as the dominant spiritual power of the times.

In contrast to the Western Empire, the Eastern Empire maintained its independence for a while. consequently tradition could preserve itself there for a longer time. the succeeding centuries nevertheless brought about such considerable losses of power externally and such radical upheavals internally that even Byzantine culture took on more and more of a medieval character.

The Emperor Constantine built a library along with the academy at Byzantium, and was particularly solicitous for Christian texts. His successors took pains to enlarge the library, so that before the great fire of 476/7 it contained a very large number of books. After the fire it was soon restored. Thereafter, however, ensued a dark period, in which intellectual life fell into decline and did not revive until after the iconoclastic controversy. During this period many ancient literary monuments were lost. those remaining—still a considerable number—were collected by the distinguished scholar Photius (d. 897/8), who in his bibliography, the *Myrobiblion*, also analyzed 280 works critically and supplied biographical notices for the authors. After him came the age of the great Byzantine encyclopedists. We do not know whether the imperial library was entirely destroyed or in what fashion it was later reconstructed, but we can assume that from this time on it continued to exist, right through the catastrophe of the Latin Crusade, up to the sack of Constantinople by the Turks.

Besides the imperial library there were ecclesiastical libraries, like those of the patriarch, and most important of all, the collections of the monasteries. During the early Christian period hermits as well as monks were already busy in the East studying and copying manuscripts, and the monasteries, following the rule of Pachomius, acquired their own book-collections. The fashion for the Middle Ages proper was set by that great reformer of Byzantine monastic life, Abbot Theodore of Studium (d. 826), whose regulations treated of the *scriptorium*, the library, and the duties of the librarian. In his abbey at Studium there developed a model school of calligraphy. Even today one can note the influence of Theodore in the monasteries of Mt. Athos, though they retain but a small remainder of their former manuscript treasures.

We have had to stop for a moment to examine the state of Byzantine culture because in what follows we shall take the opportunity in several places of referring back to it. Our main attention, however, focuses on the West, for from the book-collections which originated there in the early Middle Ages a line of development can be traced right down to the libraries of the immediate present.

The papacy considered the cultivation of the Christian tradition in the West one of its most important missions. Hence the papal library can look back upon a history of almost two thousand years. Its origins remain veiled in obscurity. We have a report dating from the beginning of the third century concerning the solicitude of one of the popes for the preservation of the acts of the martyrs. From the time when the library comes clearly into view it appears always to be closely connected with the archives. Damasus (d. 384) housed both in the Basilica of San Lorenzo. In the seventh century at the latest came its removal to the Lateran. At that time the library was often used in connection with Roman synods, and the works of the church Fathers, as well as heretical writings, were borrowed from it. In the eighth century we first encounter the important office of *bibliothecarius*, which was filled at the end of the next century by Anastasius, who deserved high praise for his translations of Greek authors. Up to this time Rome was still the great book-mart whence the whole West secured its manuscripts.

We can take it for granted that the other Italian bishops, at least from the time of Constantine, provided for libraries, large or small. Just as in the East, these were now joined by monastery libraries. St. Benedict, the founder of the Benedictine order, can hardly be counted the father of Western monastic libraries, but his rule does mention "library codices" (*codices de bibliotheca*) and enjoins the brothers "to occupy themselves with reading the sacred books" (*occupari in lectione divina*).[4] Nevertheless it was far from Benedict's mind to make scholars of the monks, and so his establishment at Monte Cassino hardly possessed an important manuscript collection at the beginning. Such a collection first came into being at Monte Cassino in the second half of the eighth century, when the monastery had become a widely influential center of learned studies and sheltered within its walls Paul the Deacon, to whom we shall refer later in another connection.

Chief credit for having made a home for Western culture in the monastery belongs to Cassiodorus. A Roman nobleman, he was a statesman in the service of Theodoric, the great King of the goths; then, about the middle of the sixth century, he withdrew into the monastery of Vivarium, founded by himself, in southern Italy. There, following Eastern models, he organized a kind of Christian academy and wrote for it his *Institutiones divinarum et saecularium litterarum* which have rightly been characterized as the scholarly rules of the monastery. They contain methodical guides to the study of Church writers as well as classical authors. At the same time special reference is constantly made to the library of the monastery, and the brothers are admonished to copy texts industriously. "Satan receives as many wounds," one passage reads, "as the monk copies words of the Lord." Just a short time before, Bishop Caesarius of Arles had directed the nuns of the convent founded by him "to make beautiful copies of the sacred books" (*libros divinos pulchre scriptitare*). But Cassiodorus was truly the first man in the West thus to aspire to a systematic collection of necessary religious and profane literary works. Even Greek texts were procured from the East and translated at Vivarium. Cassiodorus took care that the manuscripts should have a good appearance, but he laid the stress upon correctness of the texts. Such endeavors connect him with the scholars of Alexandria before him, and with Charlemagne and his learned advisers who were to come. To Cassiodorus we are indebted above all for the transmission of many literary monuments from antiquity to the Middle Ages.

At the side of Cassiodorus we must place the Spaniard, Isidore of Seville (d. 636). Probably no German tribe became so swiftly Romanized as the West Goths. The church of the Iberian Peninsula distinguished itself by a most active spiritual life up to the Arab conquest, and among the high clergy there were many ardent book-collectors. In this, however, Isidore of Seville surpassed all others. He was the greatest scholar of his time, a typical polyhistorian who brought together in his *Etymologiae* the cumulative result of contemporary knowledge and so produced the first Christian encyclopedia. His own rich library furnished the material. We can get a tolerably clear picture of it thanks to the fact that lines have come down which once adorned the bookcases or the walls, upon which also, after the ancient fashion, portrait medallions apparently were hung. There was very probably over the door an inscription reading: "Here is much that is sacred as well as much that is wordly." (*Sunt hic plura sacra, sunt mundalia plura*).[5] The inscriptions on case or wall made reference to the Bible, the Fathers, Christian poets, historians of the church, and the ancient jurists. A couplet was also devoted to the *scriptorium*.

Things developed much less propitiously in Gaul than in Spain, although this particular Roman province experienced a resurgence of late classic rhetoric and poetry during the fourth and fifth centuries, when some impressive libraries came into being (for example, that of the prefect Tonantius Ferreolus), and it enjoyed a most lively literary intercourse, as the quick spread of the *Vita S. Martini* indicates. But with the beginning of Frankish rule culture in general sank back to a lower level. A long time passed before a new rise got under way, and this even required aid from abroad, which the Irish were the first to supply.

On the Emerald Isle, which had remained untouched by the storm of tribal migrations, there had emerged a monastic life with a very special kind in which ascetic piety combined with the most diligent cultivation of art and scholarship. Here in the far Northwest there was a genuine knowledge of things Greek. Here the book was especially treasured and adorned with script and miniature which testify alike to an original sense of beauty. The designation "scribe" (*scriba*) was a title of honor, with its functions often attached to the abbotship. An astonishing missionary zeal animated the Irish, and wherever their urge to "wander about in the service of Christ" (*peregrinari pro Christo*) led them, they brought along their manuscripts.

About 590 the most important of the Irish missionaries, St. Columban, set foot on the continent and founded upon Gallic soil the abbey of Luxeuil. From here a number of other monasteries were established, among them Corbie and St. Gall. In all these establishments the arts of script and book unfolded anew. In upper Italy the monastery of Bobbio owed its origin to the Irish missionary. He himself seems to have laid the foundation of the library there, and it soon became one of the most important in Italy. It has been shown that most probably a large part of the manuscript treasures of Vivarium was transferred to Bobbio and thus preserved for posterity. The fact that most of the palimpsests known today come from Bobbio bespeaks the eagerness of Columban's disciples to enlarge their collection by copying. We have no further direct knowledge of the early period of the library. In the statutes of the abbey in the year 835 appears the decree: "The librarian shall have charge of all books, of reading, and of the scribes."[6] The oldest catalogue of the books, dating from the tenth or eleventh century, shows a collection, astonishing for its time, of over 650 volumes.

England was converted by missionaries from Ireland and, at the same time, from Rome. Under this double influence the highly gifted Anglo-Saxons appropriated and assimilated with comparative speed the material introduced by their teachers. The very first emissaries of the Pope carried manuscripts with them. Somewhat later Anglo-Saxon pilgrims traveled to Rome and returned with further treasures. Benedict Biscop, abbot of the double monastery of Wearmouth and Jarrow, made his way over the Alps five times, and on his deathbed could commend to his brothers "the most noble and copious library which he had brought from Rome" (*bibliothecam quam de Roma nobilissimam copiosissimamque advexerat*). In this abode lived and labored until 735 the Venerable Bede, who surpassed all his contemporaries as scholar and teacher.[7] He based his works upon Isidore, yet differed markedly from him. Isidore, a Roman by birth, wished to transmit the culture he had inherited to his new compatriots of alien blood. The Anglo-Saxon Bede was filled with the awe of the youthful Germans for the superior old culture. The way in which he tried to assimilate it shows already a character wholly medieval.

The Anglo-Saxons shared the missionary zeal of the Irish, and they followed the trail of their teachers, which led to the continent. St. Boniface chose as the field of his missionary endeavors a still unconverted Germany and carried thence across the sea, along with the new faith, the culture developed in England, as is shown by the insular script and insular miniature decoration of the oldest manuscripts originating east of the Rhine and north of the Main. From the beginning Boniface had at his disposal a collection of books and, as his correspondence reveals, added to it by having books sent from his native country. These he had with him up to the time of his martyrdom. The favorite establishment of this apostle to the Germans, the monastery of Fulda, possessed under its very first abbot, Sturm (d. 779), a productive *scriptorium*.

Nothing characterized the age we are describing better than this wandering and spread of manuscripts from monastery to monastery, first from South to North, then back again in the opposite direction. Then, as the eighth century faded into the ninth, the great Emperor of the Franks brought about a collection of the materials hitherto scattered throughout the West.[8]

Charlemagne's efforts were consciously directed toward raising the general standards of religion and education by combining them with the Christian heritage of late antiquity and, above all, toward bringing the clergy to be teachers of the people and giving to all the clergy a definite amount of knowledge to carry with them through life. To this end he brought to his court helpers from the neighboring lands at that time culturally more advanced. Thus there came from Italy Paul the Deacon and from England Alcuin, who brought with him across the Channel the learning of a Bede.[9] Alcuin took over direction of the palace school, which thereupon became a model for the organization of schools in all churches and monasteries. Objectives which leaders like Cassiodorus, Bede, and Boniface had pursued now became regulatory for the whole Frankish Empire. The central government saw to the setting up of *scriptoria* in religious establishments and required work correct in form and substance. A reform of writing issued from the court and book decoration adjusted itself to the new ideals of beauty. There ensued a carefully planned collecting and sifting of liturgical and scholarly literature, in which sound philological criticism according to the principle that "the source offers purer water than the stream" was applied. the best texts existed mostly in Italian manuscripts; authentic copies of these were made, and care taken to distribute them. In this way the scholars of Charlemagne's time made secure a good part of our tradition.

The seed sown by this great emperor yielded its finest fruits under his grandson, Charles the Bald, who is rightly called the first princely bibliophile of the Middle Ages. The splendid codices produced at his behest are among the finest of the age. To his

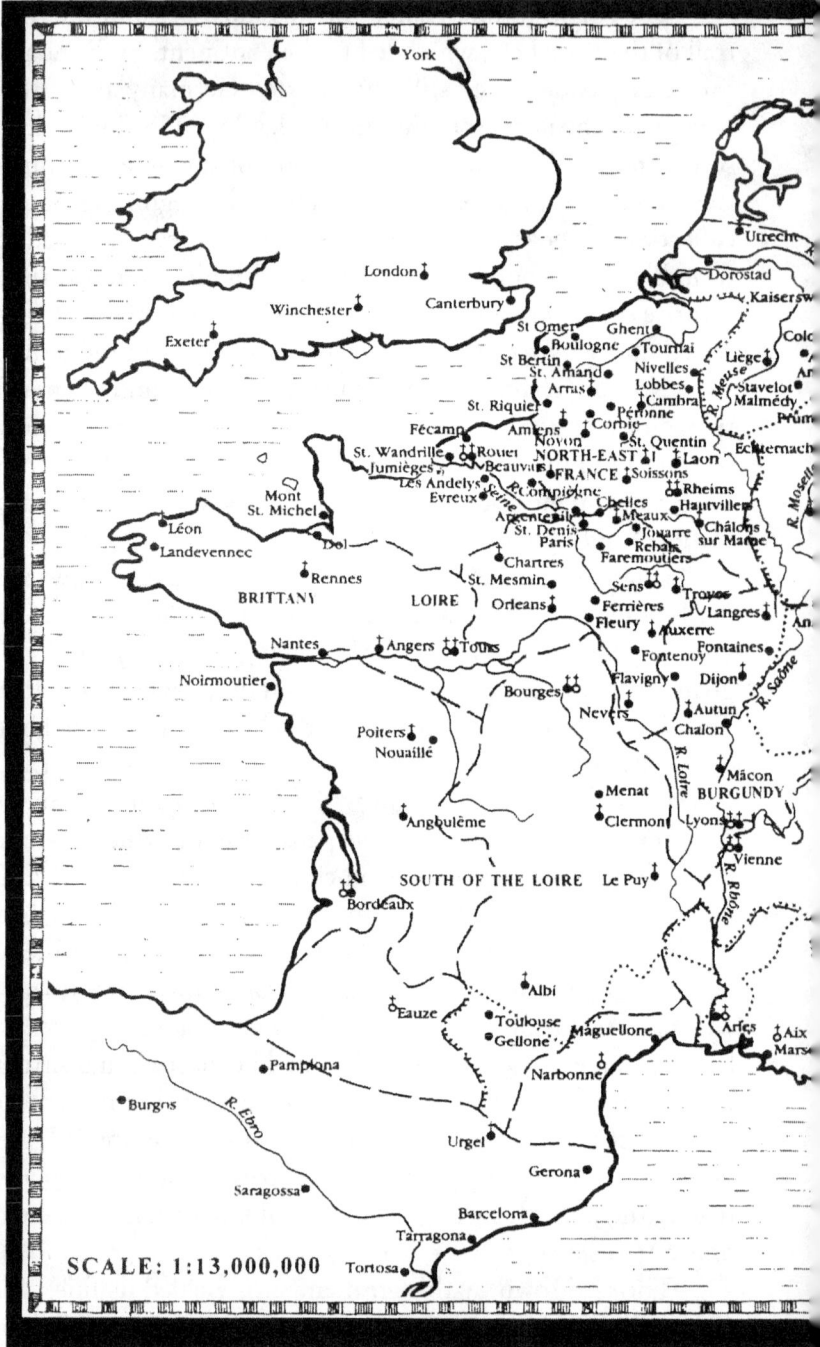

Figure 14: *Map of Europe showing the*
epsicopal and archiepsicopal sees.

MAP OF EUROPE AT THE TIME OF CHARLEMANGE

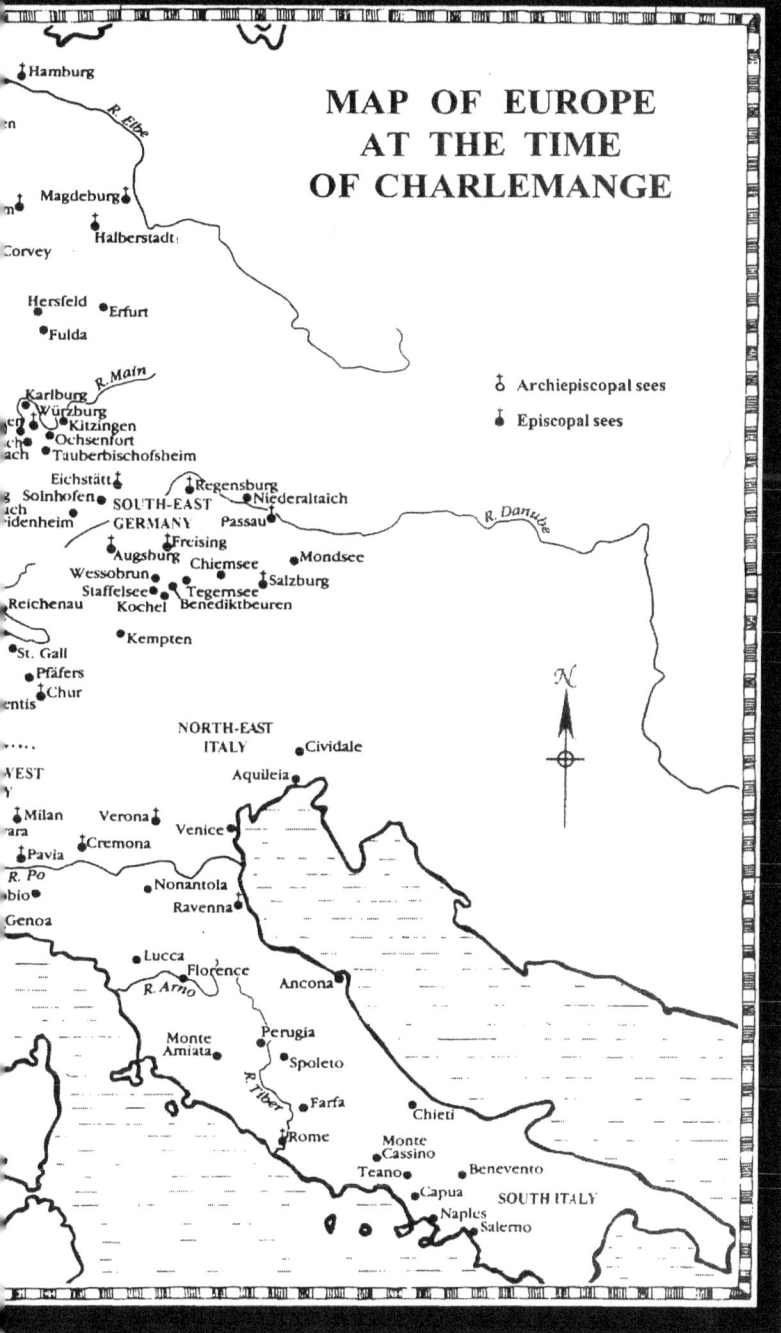

ǒ Archiepiscopal sees

ǒ Episcopal sees

Hamburg

R. Elbe

en

Magdeburg

Halberstadt

Corvey

Hersfeld Erfurt

Fulda

R. Main

Karlburg

Würzburg

Kitzingen

Ochsenfort

Tauberbischofsheim

Eichstätt

Solnhofen SOUTH-EAST

GERMANY Regensburg

Niederaltaich

idenheim Passau

GERMANY

Freising

Augsburg Chiemsee Mondsee

Wessobrun

Staffelsee Tegernsee Salzburg

Reichenau Kochel Benediktbeuren

St. Gall Kempten

Pfäfers

Chur

entis

R. Danube

NORTH-EAST
ITALY Cividale

WEST Aquileia

Milan Verona Venice

Cremona

Pavia

R. Po

bio

Genoa Nonantola

Ravenna

Lucca

Florence Ancona

R. Arno

Monte
Amiata Perugia

Spoleto

R. Tiber Farfa

Rome Chieti

Monte
Cassino

Teano Benevento

Capua SOUTH ITALY

Naples Salerno

27

palace school he called the great philosopher, John Scotus, and had him translate important works from the Greek. At that time, moreover, Abbot Lupus of Ferrières, the learned philologist, was indefatigably tracking down manuscripts of classical authors and seeking such mastery of his subject as only modern scholars, strictly speaking, have again aspired to.

The points already made concerning the tendencies and results of the so-called Carolingian Renaissance enable us to conclude that it paid particular attention also to library affairs. Charlemagne bade foreign scholars bring manuscripts with them from their native countries. To Paul the Deacon we are indebted for many classics, to Alcuin—using the words of the sources—for "the flowers of Britain" (*flores Britanniae*). The latter built the library in his abbey of St. Martin of Tours entirely on English lines, and the collection at Tours then served as a model for other ecclesiastical institutions, for now each institution felt obligated to have a library as well as a school. The palace library, however, was the center of traffic in manuscripts. Here standard texts were deposited and made available for use to anyone interested. Charlemagne was anxious to make this collection as complete and comprehensive as possible. Hence we may take it that the lines addressed to the emperor refer to the library: "Who can even enumerate the series of books which are gathered at your direction from many lands?"[10]

Besides the palace library there was yet another separate personal library of the emperor's; his grandson, Charles the Bald, also had such a library. Indeed, even Einhard, who was a layman, provided himself with a valuable collection from which Lupus of Ferrières borrowed manuscripts on the basis of a catalogue continually at his disposal. But these eloquent beginnings in the formation of private libraries soon languished, for they, like many other creations of the Carolingian Renaissance, had too far out-distanced their time to develop favorably any further. One accomplishment of the Great Emperor did endure: from his time on, libraries were part of the necessary equipment of religious institutions, especially of monasteries, throughout the large Frankish Empire.

Chapter III. The Post-Carolingian Age: The Ninth To Twelfth Centuries

The catalogue of a monastic library of the year 831 closes with the words: "Here, then, are the treasures of the monastery, here are riches feeding the soul with the sweetness of the heavenly life."[1] An equally high regard for the possession of books is shown by the regrets which a later chronicler appended to his account of the burning of a church library: "An inexpressible number of books perished, leaving us deprived of our spiritual weapons."[2] This feeling found probably its most pregnant expression in the saying formulated about 1170: "A monastery without a book-chest is like a castle without an armory."[3] Any of these citations might serve as a motto for the period of library history which extends from the ninth to the twelfth century. It was the period of undivided sway of church and monastic libraries. We shall turn our attention first to certain of these institutions so that out of individual characteristics noted here and there we may draw our general conclusions.

The foregoing chapter has already dealt with the very promising beginnings of the library of Fulda. This library did not attain its full importance till after 800, when Rabanus Maurus ruled at Fulda for four decades, first as head of the school, then of the entire abbey. He is rightly called the originator of the medieval method of teaching in Germany, for he continued Alcuin's work on East Frankish soil. Under his direction the *scriptorium* of Fulda became busy and active, to the special advantage of the library. Rabanus's own lines testify how rich and many-sided was its book collection in his time: "There you will find all that God has sent down to earth from heaven for the

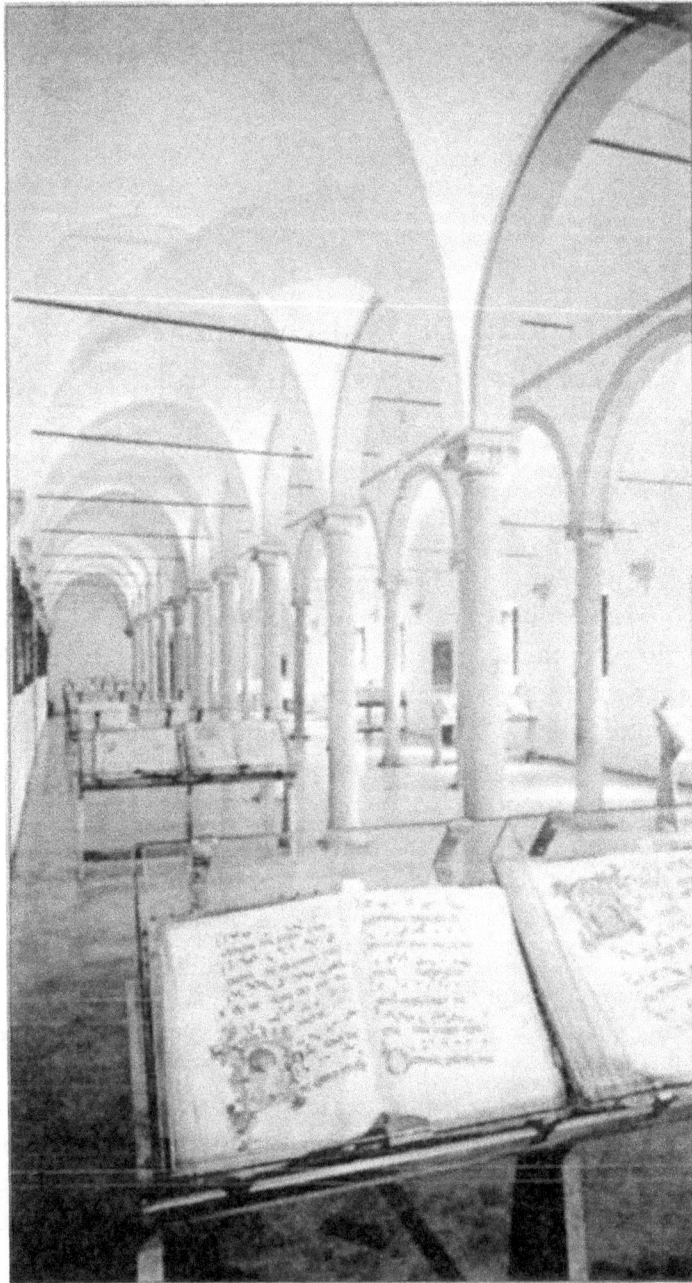

Figure 15: The library in the Monastery of San Marco, Florence.

benefit of man in the pious words of the sacred scripture and all the worldly wisdom that has been made known to the world in various ages."[4]

What Fulda was to Mainfranken, Corvey was to Saxony. Its mother abbey, Corbie, itself a colony emanating from Luxeuil, maintained probably the most productive *scriptorium* in the West at the end of the eighth century. Working there at the beginning of the following century were Adelhard and Wala, relatives of Charlemagne and members of his circle, and also the great scholar, Paschasius Radbertus. It was, in fact, the first two who in 822 transplanted the Frankish tradition to the banks of the Weser. Under the favor of the ruling dynasty Corvey developed into the intellectual capital of Saxony. Very likely the groundwork of its library derived from the collections of Corbie. In 847 a chaplain of Louis the Pious presented it with a "large supply of books" (*magna copia librorum*). Reports of its later fortunes are quite scarce, but occasionally we can augment them by deduction. Thus we know that during the tenth century Widukind wrote his valuable chronicle at Corvey, and we are justified in assuming that he drew his rich source material chiefly from the library of the abbey. Two centuries later Wibald, the close friend of Conrad III, dwelt there as abbot. His correspondence reveals his eagerness to provide the library with worthy manuscripts, especially the works of Cicero, and his pride in the results achieved.

The Carolingian Age produced two important monastic libraries in East Francia—that at Weissenburg, the home of the religious epic poet, Otfried, and (particularly noteworthy) the library at Lorsch. None of the other abbeys of the time experienced so swift and brilliant a rise. Correspondingly there occurred a large-scale development of the Lorsch manuscript collection, which in number, textual worth, and general richness of execution, easily surpassed anything to be found in its sister institutions.

Of the Swabian abbeys, St. Gall must be named first, for it may well serve as the prototype of German monastic culture for the period from the reign of Charlemagne to the beginning of the eleventh century. It had a model school, whose students graced so many episcopal seats. Of the long line of distinguished scholars and writers from St. Gall we may name the composer of sequences, Notker Balbulus; the author of the epic *Waltharius*, Ekkehard I; the philologist, Notker Labeo; and finally Ekkehard IV, the author if the *Casus S. Galli* , which give us a clear picture of the golden age of the monastery. The *scriptorium* began its activity about the middle of the eighth century. The true founder of the library was the abbot Grimald (841-872) along with his successor Hardmut. Right up to the eleventh century busy copyists and liberal benefactors such as Bishop Salomon of Constance saw to its growth. We know the names of the librarians, among them Notker Balbulus; we have reliable information on the richness of the collection from catalogues which have survived; we even possess a calendar, begun in the ninth and carried on during the following centuries, specifying the lives of the saints and the passions for each day which were to be found in the library. Scholars know much less that is exact about the Asatian abbey of Murbach than they do about St. Gall. Nevertheless, a list dating from the middle of the ninth century reveals what books were already in its possession at that time and how diligent an effort was being made to acquire more.

A third center of religious life in Swabia was Reichenau, which carried on a very brisk exchange of manuscripts with neighboring St. Gall and repeatedly supplied Murbach with books. Since its founding the abbots had been industrious book collectors, but the golden age of the Reichenau library too arrived with the rule of Charlemagne, Reginbert easily the most important librarian of his time, was active there until 846. He himself produced important texts of sacred and profane authors and supervised the work of industrious students; he garnered codices from near and far, from Italy and the West Frankish Kingdom; and in his catalogues he rendered careful accounts of the treasures assembled. In his day the library numbered over 400 volumes. That its contents resembled other monastic libraries mentioned above should not be regarded as an accident; for these libraries were built up on the plan of the emperor's palace library and with its support, and yet each shone forth in its own light, and together they reflected the spirit and the learning of Alcuin and his school. The scholarly impulse remained at high pitch for a long time at Reichenau; about the end of the tenth century, however, it began to wane, while the reputation of its school of painters became all the greater. Even though the other monasteries, especially Fulda, produced many beautiful examples of the fine art of bookmaking about the time of the emperor Otto the Great, to the miniaturists of Richenau went the commissions not only of princes and bishops but also of the imperial court, and even of the Pope at Rome.

With the opening of the eleventh century Regensburg assumed the leadership in illumination in Germany. We can observe how a general upswing among Bavarian monasteries set in after the terrific threat of Hungarian invasion was averted in the great Battle of the Lechfeld. One of the leading personages of the time was Bishop Wolfgang of Regensburg. To St. Emmeram as the abbot he called Ramwold, who busied himself with reviving the abbey, "most of all by the cultivation of books" *(maxime in librorum cultibus),* so that the catalogue drawn up under his direction contained over 500 titles. A few decades later the great calligrapher Othlo worked at St. Emmeram. His unusual autobiography enumerates the long series of manuscripts which he produced, and the examples which have survived justify the recognition which his contemporaries tendered him.

From Regensburg Gozbert was sent to the monastery of Tegernsee to be abbot. There his work resembled that of Ramwold at St. Emmeram. The correspondence of the learned master of his school, Froumund, gives us an insight into the many pains he took to acquire texts to be copied for Tegernsee; for the same purpose, in return, parts of his own library were loaned. In the following years the reputation of the monastery as a center for the production of manuscripts mounted. Even Emperor Frederick Barbarossa longed to possess a missal and a lectionary made there because the Tegernsee monks were reputed to be "fine scribes" *(bon scriptores)*. We are best informed about the *scriptorium* of Michelsberg at Bamberg, as the librarian, Burchard (d. 1149), has left a kind of history of the collection entrusted to him. Here we learn what book-stock he found was to begin with and everything that was added by gift, purchase, and copying, and we are even told the names of the individual copyists and the division of work among them. Michelsberg apparently also produced manuscripts for export. What an intense intellectual life ruled at the abbey in this period can be appreciated from the diversity of the book stock and no less from the fact that the most important universal chronicle of the time originated there.

During the period which now concerns us distinguished libraries were not wanting in Germany in cathedrals but, on the whole, they lagged behind monastic libraries in importance. It is true that the cultural endeavors of Charlemagne's co-workers affected the one as well as the other: at this time Archbishop Lullus of Mainz and his colleagues, Hildebald of Cologne and Arno of Salzburg, did make very useful beginnings; nor were these collection at all neglected by their successors. But, as history shows, the German bishops of the tenth to the twelfth centuries, in addition to their religious duties, participated whole-heartedly in imperial politics. Hence they had little leisure for their special problems as leaders of cultural life. An outstanding exception was Bernward of Hildesheim (d. 1022), who made his residence a place for the cultivation of art and knowledge. He also assembled, in the words of his librarian and biographer Thangmar, "a large library of codices of the sacred authors as well as the philosophers" *(copiosam bibliothecam tam divnorum quam philosophicorum codicum)*.

If we were to portray the development of collections in other countries with the same minute detail as the German, we should be merely piling up details without getting any clearer insight into the nature and structure of the library of the time. For, during this whole period Germany was the leading power in Europe, not only politically but culturally as well. It will be enough, therefore, to point out by a few characteristic examples how libraries everywhere, even far from the borders of Germany, were on the upgrade, especially where an intensive monastic life unfolded anew or revived.

To begin with the South, this is true of the mother abbey of Monte Cassino. After long decline it blossomed forth again during the eleventh century and under Abbot Desiderius regained its former renown. During this period the characteristic Cassino script and miniature work reached their highest consummation, and the bringing together of rich new manuscript collections generated scholarly activity that even acted as a model for work outside the monastery walls. At about this same time Abbot Jerome of Pomposa was attracting the attention of northern Italy by reforming his abbey and having a large number of codices made for its library.

From the tenth century on, the Order of Cluny had been giving aim and direction to ecclesiastical France.[5] Its founder, Odo, had already brought to Cluny with him 100 manuscripts, and one of his successors, Majolus, first as librarian and later as abbot, had had the monks ply their copying industrially. At the end of our period the library contained about 600 volumes. The other abbeys reformed under the influence of Cluny, for example Fleury-sur-Loire, also acquired considerable stores of books. The twelfth-century rules of the pious Order of St. Victor of Paris deserve closer attention, for they contain a separate section devoted to the duties of the librarian. Such an interest in books as appears herein was in keeping with the general scholarly zeal of the Victorines. Their institution is rightly considered one of the seeds from which grew the University of Paris.

The spirit and discipline of Cluny pressed on across the Channel to England. Under William the Conqueror, Lanfranc, Archbishop of Canterbury, led the reform movement. He revived the library of Christ Church and issued general orders for regular distribution of books in the monasteries of England. One of his relatives, Paul, abbot of St. Albans, organized the *scriptorium* there, made over to it permanent sources of income, attracted scribes from outside, and at the same time provided the library with valuable gifts. From then on to the end of the twelfth century, almost all the heads of the abbey concerned themselves with the *scriptorium* and the library. The manuscripts thus assembled were one of the conditions which made possible the great progress in the writing of history at St. Albans in the following century.

What most differentiates the medieval library from the ancient as well as the modern library is the meagerness of its book-stock. Catalogues of medieval libraries contain at most a few hundred entries.[6] In this connection, too, it must be observed that often several titles are combined in one codex. The whole literature available to the age—that is to say, the Christian writings and the surviving fragments of antiquity, together with the scholarly and devotional works brought out from the ninth to the twelfth century—could actually be contained in a number of volumes as small as this.

If a new monastery was founded, as a rule it received the basic part of its book stock, or at least the necessary liturgical manuscripts from its mother abbey. Then the collection grew by means of gifts from the most varied sources, from religious and secular circles, as a result of which these benefactors were usually received into the brotherhood of prayer. Other material was brought by newly admitted monks or by youths who attended the monastery school. The bequests of dead brothers also proved to be quite fruitful. Purchases could be made only with great difficulty, for the value of manuscripts was extraordinarily high. Frequently we hear that whole plots of land—for example, vineyards—had to be paid as a price for manuscripts. Hence it became customary to make the necessary funds available by special endowments and by setting aside permanent taxes or rents.

Very lively exchange of manuscripts took place among the various religious institutions. For one thing, it made easier the exchange of duplicates; more often, however, it was a means of procuring texts which were then used as models for copying. Everywhere we have found firmly established the closest connection between library and *scriptorium*. Indeed it is not too much to assert that the contents and growth of the former depended essentially upon the industry and productivity of the latter. This activity involved not merely making copies and ornamenting them with miniatures; the monks had to provide and prepare all the necessary materials themselves—parchment and quill, ink and dye, boards and leather. That no one thought his position too exalted for such work reveals the whole monastic point of view. In hope of reward in heaven, the monks copied for weeks, months, years. In return, however , the merit of this activity was also stressed on every suitable occasion.[7]

We can now understand why the monks valued and guarded their manuscripts just as they did the treasures of the monastery. To their material worth and their importance as scholarly equipment was added the spiritual reason that they bore witness to work pleasing to God. The brothers were enjoined to use them with the greatest care and foresight; the manuscripts were proudly provided with marks of ownership, and attempts were made to guard against loss by inscribing so-called book-curses. These threats of temporal and mundane punishment can be traced far back into earlier centuries. During our period, executed sometimes in prose, sometimes in verse, the developed into a type of literature of their own.

A surer safeguard against theft than the book-curse, however, was afforded by careful and orderly administration of the library. This duty devolved upon the *armarius* or *librarius,* an important official in the abbey, who often had still other functions to discharge. In many places, for example, he held the office of *precentor* or *custos* at the same time. Quite naturally, he always had direction—or at least participated in the

The Memory of Mankind

direction—of the *scriptorium*. The extent of his library duties proper depended upon the size of the library in his trust.

In the earliest times, and also later, manuscripts were kept together with the treasures in a safe place, for example the sacristy or one of the chapels. Sometimes they were kept with the deeds and documents of the archives. If the book stock was small, one or more chests or cupboards sufficed, of which some stood apart and others were sunk into the wall, just as we noticed in ancient times. If the number of books increased, however, they required special quarters. These have not been preserved from the Carolingian Age, but we do have the so-called architectural plan of St. Gall, a model plan for the layout of a large monastery of the time. In this plan "the library is a building which quite bespeaks the sacristy in location and size and stands against the eastern side of the presbytery. In consists of two stories. The lower is furnished as a *scriptorium* ...the upper... is used for the storage of books." We know that at a later date manuscripts were stored by the Cistercians in rooms set apart near the refectory. Of Tegernsee it is reported that in the new church being erected there "the library is located above the basilica itself" (*super eandem basilicam armaria locatur*). Quite often the liturgical codices appointed for public worship were set apart from the other books; often also the books were divided into an inner collection, which was intended for the members of the monastery, and an outer collection belonging to the school; and finally a distinction was made between reference books and books for circulation.

The statutes of some orders contained strict regulations concerning the procedure for lending books. On an appointed day of the year the brothers assembled in the chapter house. There those who had borrowed books the last time were called by name and required to return them. Then the business of lending books for the next year proceeded. All this was under the direction of the *librarius*, who also had to keep lists of the books lent. We have been concerned here only with the lending of books to members of the monastery, but lending was not confined to these alone, as we have several times indicated above. For books lent outside, however, a receipt and a deposit were required. Reginbert of Reichenau was already admonishing the brothers that "no work was to be given to anyone to take outside unless he had first given a pledge or at least left security that he would return safe to this house what he had received."[8] Since, however, even precautions of this kind could not always prevent abuse and loss, it came to pass toward the end of our period that the rules of the monastery entirely forbade lending books outside the institution.

One of the duties of the *librarius* was to classify and take inventory of the books. Catalogues of the great Carolingian monastic libraries, which, as we have seen, contained very similar manuscript holdings, also show a fairly uniform subject-grouping.

At the beginning stand the sacred writings; the Church Fathers, up to the "modern masters" (*magistri moderni*) come next, arranged by author; then comes the remainder of the sacred literature and the profane literature, including ancient pagan writers, also divided into definite subject-groups.[9] On the basis of evidence afforded by the late Middle Ages, we can assume that the arrangement of the books followed the same system and that, therefore, the Carolingian inventories can already be spoken of as shelf-lists. One the other hand, there is no trace at this time of the later custom of placing manuscripts on desks instead of keeping them in chests and then guarding against their being removed at will by the use of chains. The earliest scattered references to "chained books" (*libri catenati*) belong to the following centuries.

The internal arrangement of the monastic library from the tenth to the twelfth century we can sum up briefly. Surviving catalogues differ widely in quality, and often leave much to be desired in completeness and exactitude. Not infrequently the arrangement is determined simply by order of accession, or no particular order is aimed at. Whether it became customary at this time or even earlier to provide each volume with a location mark is for further research to determine. In general, one gets the impression that the post-Carolingian development of the medieval library showed no further essential progress. Such progress ensued again only when Scholasticism made its influence felt upon library matters.

Figure 16: Line engraving of a chained book.

Chapter IV. The Late Middle Ages

We have seen how, in monasteries and other religious institutions, manuscript treasures were collected and united into libraries; how industrious monks steadily enlarged these spiritual riches, produced text after text by careful copying, and adorned them with beautiful miniatures; and how they thus saw to it that this tradition never lapsed, but rather that the heritage of ancient times was handed down to posterity. During this whole period ecclesiastical institutions were indeed the only places where the conditions favorable to intellectual pursuits could be found. The Church acquired a kind of monopoly upon education; knowledge became entirely clericalized; the Latin of the scholars held the field alone as the literary language. We can hardly even say that laymen took any independent part of their own in the great cultural activities of the day.

Figure 17: Brother Lawrence, a monk of Durham, in a codex of 1149–1154.

It was not until the later Middle Ages that a definite change came about. The laity freed themselves from the intellectual tutelage of the Church, and first to do this were naturally the nobility. They developed a characteristically aristocratic mode of life, created for themselves courtly poesy and genteel light reading. Then came the rise of the middle class in the cities. As trade and manufacture boomed, as knowledge of reading and writing became more and more widespread, there awoke in the middle class a desire for culture and instruction. This need was satisfied by a semi-scientific and popular literature which made use of the vernacular and swelled into an ever mightier stream.

Figure 18: A Premonstratensian monk, 14th century manuscript.

The new monastic orders, Franciscans and Dominicans, settled in the cities. No longer did they lead a contemplative existence removed from the world, but instead stepped into the thick of life, made their influence felt by sermon and teaching, and gave new direction to knowledge. It was through their cooperation, in fact, that the great universities arose toward the end of the Middle Ages—foremost among them Bologna, the home of legal studies, and Paris, the stronghold of Scholastic theology and philosophy. These set a pattern for the other *studia generalia* in Italy, France, England, and Germany.[1] These brief remarks concerning the new orientation of Western culture should suffice to justify the division of the subject-matter of this chapter. It will attempt to answer the following questions: First, what was the later fate of the monastic library? Second, what kind of libraries do we find among the aristocracy and later among the middle class? Finally, how did the universities meet their needs in the way of books?

In many an old Benedictine abbey the religious and scholarly spirit weakened with time and with it vanished also the urge to copy and collect. Indeed, in many places we can observe a complete disintegration of monasteries and their accommodations. The library fell into neglect; the manuscripts were pledged and sold for a trifle. There was hence full justification for the loud laments we already find in Dante in the thirteenth century, for those to which Richard de Bury was giving utterance in his *Philobiblon* during the following century, and, finally, for those which are contained in the descriptions of the Humanists of the fifteenth century—even though the latter are exaggerated. Nevertheless we must not make these indictments too general. Let us but call to mind the great manuscript possessions acquired by religious foundations and monasteries toward the end of the Middle Ages and the magnificent choir-books which the fourteenth and fifteenth centuries have handed down to us. In this very period we have reports of the reorganizing and building of libraries, and we know also of a number of able and zealous librarians, such as Heinrich von Ligerz of Einsiedeln, treatment of whose work has recently been found worthy of a monograph.[2] As far as Germany in particular is concerned, the Council of Constance instigated a reform of Benedictine monasteries. Wherever this took effect, it led to a revival of scholarly enthusiasm. In the South, Melk operated as a model for Austria, Bavaria, and Swabia; in central and northern Germany it was the Congregation of Bursfeld,[3] founded in 1433. In the case of all these reformed monasteries we have some testimony about well-kept and well-supported libraries, and to some extent there is a justifiable presumption of their existence.

The other monastic orders must also be considered. We hear, for example, of cultivation of libraries among the Carthusians and the Augustinian Friars. The Franciscans quickly got over the dislike of the founder of their order for books and study. The scholarly activity of the English Minorities developed with particularly fruitful results. They possessed rich collections in London and Oxford. From the fifteenth century there has been preserved the *Registrum librorum Angliae*, a sort of union catalogue of 85 authors compiled on the basis of a general inquiry which the Franciscan organization carried out in 160 church libraries.[4] Even more universal was the ardor of the Dominicans, who, as is well known, set up a system of scholarly instruction. If they assembled their libraries from a practical viewpoint and placed less value upon the external appearance than upon the contents of the manuscripts, this merely expressed their fundamental principle that utility should precede curiosity. The fifth master general of the order, Humbert de Romanis (1254-63) already devoted a whole section of his *Instructio officialium* to the *librarius*. This official must take care that there be appropriate space, a readily comprehensible classification, catalogues and shelf-marks and a loan-book, and he must see to yearly inventory, and finally to building up the book stock. From the fourteenth century have come down the provisions of several general chapters regarding monastic libraries; from the following century we have the library rules of various Dominican convents.

A word about Arab-Spanish library affairs must precede treatment of our second question, for western Christian libraries appear to have been influenced somewhat by them. The historical mission which Islam fulfilled in transmitting the corpus of Greek and Eastern literature to Europe is often spoken of. A goodly part of this scholarly achievement consisted, of course, in gathering and assimilating the knowledge accumulated by conquered peoples. For this reason books and writing assumed special importance there, and libraries were fitted out in the most lavish manner. Unfortunately they have not as yet been carefully studied, so that we must content ourselves with a few suggestions which carry no certainty.

The great rise of literary and scientific activity in the Islamic world set in toward the end of the eighth century. It was promoted by the manufacture of paper, introduced at that time from the Far East, which provided a cheap material for the production of books. The libraries of the Eastern Roman Empire seem to have been used as models in building. Thus we hear that Harun-al-Raschid founded a library in Bagdad and received manuscripts from Byzantium and elsewhere as tribute.[5] His son Mamun (d. 833) was an even more ardent collector. He is credited with having instigated the scholarly enterprise of translating the masterpieces of Greek and Oriental literature

Figure 19: Dominican monks in their scriptorium, 14th century.

into Arabic. In addition to Bagdad, there were libraries at Kufa and Basra; in fact, before long all the larger mosques, as well as the universities established throughout the caliphate, acquired their own book collections. Of Persia there are similar reports. A traveler at the end of the tenth century tells of having come across a large collection in the palace of a Buyid prince at Shiraz; another traveler at the beginning of the thirteenth century, as many as twelve libraries founded in Merv.

The libraries of the Near East had competition in North Africa (e.g. Cairo and Alexandria) and above all in Spain. In the great period of Morrish culture there seem to have been about 70 public libraries on the Iberian peninsula. Caliph Hakam II (d. 976) is famous for having founded the grandest institution. He united the libraries of his father and brother with his own and had them set up in his palace at Cordova. He gathered about him scholars, copyists, and miniaturists, and sent agents to the Orient in order to get as complete as possible collection of its literature. Even if descriptions of the number of volumes, the size of the catalogues, and the whole library structure are colored by Oriental fantasy, nevertheless they presuppose a clear idea of such an institution—and that in a time when the Christian West know only monastic libraries. Toledo afterwards became distinguished for its abundance of libraries, just as it also became the center for the translation of Arabic literature into western languages. Later on Granada also achieved eminence. Along with public libraries there seems to have been a large number of splendid private collections. Bibliophily was fashionable among the aristocracy, and even the less well-to-do were moved by a love of books.

As is well known, the Hohenstaufen Emperor Frederick II had close relations with the Islamic world and eagerly promoted the translation of Arabic literature. Presumably he was stimulated by this to the planning of his own library. At any rate, he was one of the first western rulers to possesses a large library, of which he boasted in his letter to the University of Bologna. As for the other great thirteenth-century ruler in whose reign medieval culture in France reached its highest development, his biographer says of Louis IX: "He heard it said of a certain sultan of the Saracens that he had diligent search made for all kinds of books which might be necessary to Saracen philosophers, and had these copied at his own expense and kept them in his library so that scholars could have a supply of these books whenever they needed them"[6] In accordance with this ideal the king had placed in the Sainte Chapelle a collection of the Church Fathers which he himself diligently studied and willingly permitted others to use. We may call Louis the founder of the Bibliotheque du Roi, but a large share of the credit must go to the great scholar, Vincent of Beauvais. The king also ordered handsome Bibles and psalters. In growing number the artists engaged in producing them belonged to the lay classes. From then on there developed in Paris the craft of illuminators (*elumineurs*), which was organized as a guild and which made the capital of France the European center of this splendid book-industry.

In his will Louis IX made over the library to four religious establishments. His successors showed little inclination to book-collecting, but a change came about with the art-loving House of Valois of the fourteenth century. Charles V inherited quite a few books from his father; others he acquired by purchase; but by far the largest number were commissioned. In this way over 900 manuscripts were assembled which Christine de Pisan might well describe as "the noble library...of all the most noteworthy volumes which have been compiled by sovereign authors...volumes which have been compiled by sovereign authors...of all the sciences, most beautifully written and richly adorned."[7] Charles, too, was proud of his collection and inscribed marks of ownership in many volumes with his own hand. They satisfied his taste for luxury as well as his live desire for knowledge, for he had a large number of translations made into French—among others some of the works of Aristotle and Augustine. In 1367/8 the main part of his book treasures was moved to one of the towers of the Louvre and distributed in three rooms; the rest remained in various castles. Mallet, the *valet de chambre* so highly esteemed by Louis, undertook the direction of the library and drew up an inventory with valuable details. The king willingly lent books to others and was happy to give some as gifts. Nevertheless, the main body of the collection remained intact and even grew considerably under Charles's successors. The English occupation of the fifteenth century brought about its downfall.[8]

During the reign of Charles V, love of luxurious books spread among the French nobility; in particular the members of the royal house embraced the habit. The most brilliant patron of the *enlumineurs* was Charles's brother, Duke John of Berry. He expended tremendous sums and engaged the foremost artists, so that his splendid Gothic codices and charming books of hours are among the most beautiful produced by contemporary miniaturists. The dukes of Burgundy maintained the Valois tradition till almost the end of the fifteenth century. The third duke, Philip the Good, desired to possess "the richest and noblest library in the world" (*la plus riche et noble librairie du monde*), and kept continually at work a whole group of literati, translators, calligraphers, and illuminators, among them the astonishingly productive and versatile Aubert. The Burgundian library maintained a steadfast character during the entire period. Renaissance influences from Italy were slow to make themselves felt, as, for example, under Charles the Bold, who longed to vie in repute with ancient heroes.

In the fourteenth century there was in France another splendid princely library, that of the Pope at Avignon. Recent studies have made clear the cultural significance of the papal court's being situated there at the time, and have pointed out the strong concentration of scholars and writers, artists and craftsmen from all neighboring lands. We have spoken before of the beginnings of the papal library at Rome. Its later career is largely shrouded in darkness. Only the inventory which Boniface VIII had compiled in 1295 has survived, and this lists about 500 volumes, among them over 30 Greek codices. On the removal of the papacy to Avignon, however, the library remained behind in Italy and there met destruction. The founder of the new collection was Pope John XXII (1316-34), who purchased an unusually large number of items, while his two successors had more manuscripts made. A very productive source of growth was the right of escheat, in accordance with which the estate of every divine who died at the *curia* fell to the papal exchequer. In this way the number of volumes grew in time to 1500. They were divided into the library proper, the private library of the Pope, and the repository, which was set aside to provide for religious institutions. In many respects, for example in brilliant decoration of manuscripts, the papal collection resembled that of Charles V. But in Avignon there was less light reading and fewer transla-

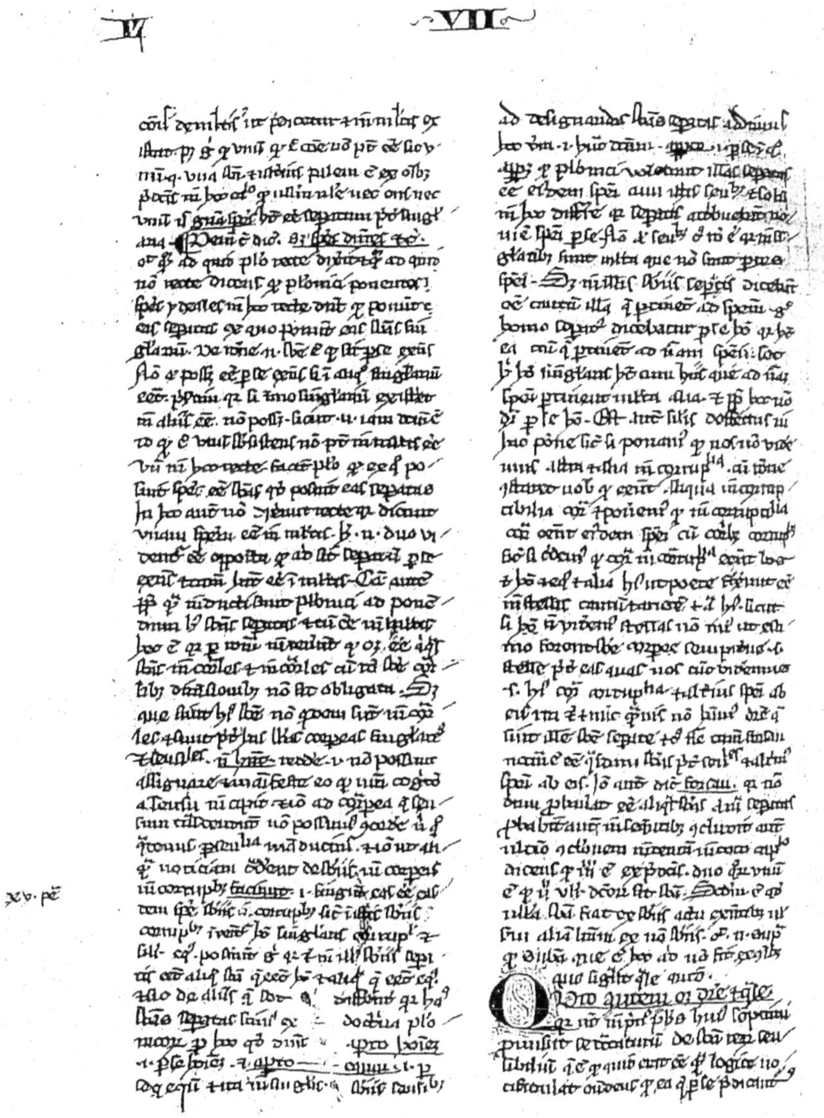

Figure 20: The Bible, from a manuscript written by Dominican monks, Paris, 13th century.

tions. Because of its great wealth of scholarly, theological, and philosophical works we might compare it with the library of the Sorbonne, which will concern us further below. Still, it differed from the later in that in contained much literature on law and church government to meet the needs of the papal court.

In those days Prague was under the influence of Paris and Avignon. King Charles IV of the house of Lusemburg, assisted by his remarkable chancellor, Johann von Neumarkt, successfully strove to make his court a rallying point of science and art. Until nearly the end of the fourteenth century the school of Prague held the leadership in manuscript illumination in central Europe. Many other German princes too, such as Ludwig III, the elector Palatine, as well as members of the nobility, embraced the grand cult of books. In general, however, they do not bear comparison with their French compeers. To make up for this, Germany surpassed her western neighbors in developing book-collections in towns.

During the fourteenth and fifteenth centuries the prestige and influence of the German city grew steadily, so that it impressed its spirit upon the whole epoch. A new literature was written for the middle class and eagerly collected. About 1300 the poet Hugo von Trimberg, author of *Der Renner*, was already boasting of his 200 books. Toward the end of the period, we find in almost every middle-sized city libraries of varying size owned by the clergy, the aldermen, the physician, the school-master, and also by some of the patricians and their wives. At the newly established municipal schools probably only individual teachers possessed the necessary books. On the other hand, there were in many places aldermanic libraries, intended for the use of the town clerk and attorneys or of the town physician. Many of these collections originated through private initiative. Before long there even came to be institutions of a public character, although they are not comparable to those which the next chapter will point out as creations of Italian Renaissance. Thus Canon Johann von Kirchdorff in 1399 bequested his home and its books to the inhabitants of Alzey/ and likewise the pastor of Ulm, Neithard (d. 1439), left to the public his library, which was then, under the supervision of his family, placed in a separate room near the minister and thrown open to use.

The demands of a public avid for the reading matter were filled by paid copyists. At first these were still clerics; later laymen predominated. In the fifteenth century the book-trade also spread through Germany. Books were sold from stalls near the principal church, or buyers frequented the great book-fairs, especially the one at Frankfurt.[9] In southern Germany the town of Hagenau, where Diebold Lauber started a flourishing venture in the production of manuscripts, became especially important. In the Netherlands and North Germany the Brothers of the Common Life supplied the market with books. From the very first their founder, Gerhard Groot, focused their interest upon books. The "Broeders van de penne," as they were called, began by taking care of the needs of their own libraries, then more and more they produced books predominantly for sale in order to defray the expenses of their houses. They turned out both large and costly choir-books and also popular devotional tracts, many in the German language. In charge of the writing-room was the *scripturarius*, whose directions the *rubricator* and the *litator* had to follow; then there was the *librarius*, whose duty it was to supervise the library. For all these the statutes contained exact instructions.

The *stationarii* occupied themselves with the manufacture and sale of scholarly literature. They were to be found in most universities—largest in number, as is easy to understand, at Paris, so that Richard de Bury was able to describe the book-mart there as a "flourishing garden of the world's books" (*virens viridarium universorum voluminum*). The aris book-trade was under strict control of the university authorities. On the other hand—these authorities did not bother to set up a university library, a situation partly connected with the fact that the University of Paris, like the other earliest universities, did not originate in an act establishing it, but rather grew quite slowly by the consolidation of various educational institutions.[10] The task of supplying necessary books to teachers and students was left instead to the individual colleges or student halls, those institutions of a semi-religious character which in most universities were formed on the plan of the Franciscan and Dominican religious houses.

About 1250 Robert de Sorbonne, Louis IX's chaplain, founded the college named after him, which has now become so famous. He bequeathed to it his own library, and gifts poured in thereafter so quickly and in such volume that the library of the Sorbonne soon far outdistanced the other libraries of the University of Paris. The bequests of individual scholars numbered usually about 100 volumes, once even 300, and among the benefactors were Germans, Englishmen, Italians, and Spaniards. Many authors made a practice of depositing their original manuscripts at the Sorbonne. There was also money available from legacies and the sale of duplicates with which to buy or commission manuscripts. In 1290 the library numbered over 1000 volumes, in 1338 over 1700. Theology and philosophy formed the chief contingent. The Fellows of the college were provided with keys, the remaining members of the university being allowed to enter under certain conditions, while strangers needed an introduction. There were two divisions—the great (*magna*) and the small (*parva*). In the former, codices frequently used lay chained upon 26 desks. The contents of the latter division, duplicates and material seldom used, might be loaned, and often indeed for quite a long time. A pledge was required, however, usually consisting of another book. There were several administrative posts manned by Fellows of the university. In addition to the Sorbonne there came into being in Paris up to the end of the Middle Ages about 50 more colleges. Each had its book collection, large or small.

The organization of all these libraries did not differ essentially from that of church and monastic libraries, even though the student halls, as we have already seen, were patterned on the whole after the establishments of the mendicant orders. Compared with the typical library of the preceding period, however, the tendency to practical scholarship was more pronounced. Thus the Scholastic studies which were pursued at the university and in which the Dominicans took an outstanding role, led to a better organization of the book-collection. This organization was governed by the system of scholarly instruction (liberal arts and faculties) as it had developed from ancient times through Cassiodorus and Isidore down to Alcuin and Rabanus Maurus. Even before the thirteenth century it revealed itself occasionally in the classification of books, but for the first time now it was laid down as a principle. Librarians, however, did not consider themselves inescapably tied down to the given scheme, but varied it in many ways and added new divisions whenever the accumulation of manuscripts forced them to it. The different classes were, as a rule, placed coordinately next to one another, but not yet reduced to a system of main and sub-classes, something which first came about in the seventeenth century.

It is hard to make a general statement concerning the method of keeping manuscripts, especially as differences in individual countries and orders must be reckoned with, for literary references are not clearly understandable, and though many church and college libraries have survived, their arrangement has frequently been altered. I believe this is all that may be said: along with the older practice of depositing the volumes in chests, in the later Middle Ages the new method of keeping them, namely the lectern system, seems to have entrenched itself more and more. The library, then, contained a row of desks, each having several shelves on which rested the books, chained to iron bars.[11] Desks, shelves, and codices were marked with letters or numbers, and besides this the faculties were sometimes distinguished by color. The inventory took the form of a shelf-list; to this alphabetical indexes were sometimes added. At its fullest the description of an individual volume contained the titles of the works found therein, the *incipit* and *explicit*, press-mark, provenance and price, and sometimes, in addition, details of the kind of script and general make-up.

At the Italian universities, as for example in Bologna, there were of course libraries, but apparently they had no greater significance, perhaps because there the *stationarii* had instituted a comprehensive lending system. It was different in Germany. At Prague the oldest university, the Collegium Carolinum, was founded by Charles IV in 1366 and was quickly well supplied with books. The College of the Bohemian Nation, created soon thereafter, immediately provided for a library. Similar libraries of student halls are to be found also at the other contemporary universities. Of their number the institution founded by the scholarly and industrious collector, Amplonius of Erfurt (d. 1434/5), deserves special mention, for even today the Amplonian manuscripts constitute the chief treasures of the library there. If, then, matters at first developed about as they had in France, the Germans, on the other hand, early took a further step and set up faculty libraries, especially that of the Faculty of Arts. This was first done at Heidelberg, and in fact soon after the year in which the university was founded (1386). At about the same time a common library was created there for all the faculties.

Thomas Cobham, Bishop of Worcester, paved the way for a general university library at Oxford as early as 1327, but as a consequence of various difficulties, it did not begin to function properly until 1412. We have reports of the general university library (*communis libraria universitatis*) at Cambridge from the beginning of the fifteenth century. On the other hand, there were libraries of religious orders and college libraries at both universities considerably earlier. Richard de Bury (d. 1345) planned the most ambitious enterprise for Oxford, though it went unrealized in his time. He had been the tutor of Edward III; later he rose to the rank of Bishop of Durham and Chancellor of England, and made several trips to the continent on important diplomatic missions. De Bury is considered not one of the outstanding scholars, but one of the most passionate bibliophiles of his day. Like the French princes, he gathered about him miniaturists, copyists, revisers, and book-binders; he dealt with sellers of manuscripts in France, Germany, and Italy, and poured out gold with a lavish hand as often as he visited the Paris book-market. In answer to numerous attacks upon his love of books, shortly before his death he composed the *Philobiblon*, which is still read with pleasure today. In it he intones a rapturous hymn of praise to the book, exalts it as the source of eternal truth, the light of the faithful soul, the weapon bestowed by God to combat all heresy. The peculiar charm of the apology consists in the fact that it contains a sound library theory—though clothed in medieval garb—and above all in its lively and original portrayal of the personality of its author and of his collector's ardor.

Chapter V. The Renaissance

The preceding chapter closed with Richard de Bury; at the head of this one we must put Petrarch. Although he was only slightly younger than the Englishman, and even came to know de Bury personally, he belonged to quite a different culture. While de Bury remained firmly rooted in Scholasticism, Petrarch became the founder of Italian Humanism.

Petrarch turned his back intentionally on the Middle Ages and fixed his attention on classical antiquity, which he perceived not as dead past but as living present. Consequently Cicero was the determining influence on his literary production as well as on his mode of life. He was possessed by a passionate fondness for classical authors. In order to acquire their writings he used all the means at his disposal, including wide travels and his many personal connections. Texts which could not be obtained by purchase or gift he

Figure 21: Petrarch at his writing-desk, 15th century.

copied himself or had copied for him. The material thus assembled was eagerly studied and provided with marginal notes. A whole dialogue in Petrarch's *De remediis utriusque fortunae*[1] rails against the mere accumulation of unread books. He placed great value upon beauty in the make-up of the manuscript, but purity of text seemed to him even more important. The library was guarded by his servants like a shrine, and he himself kept up an active acquaintance with his books, just as if they were friends capable of talking. "Books," he once wrote, "heartily delight us, speak to us, counsel us, and are joined to us, as it were, by a living and active relationship."[2] One morning he was found dead in his study, head sunk upon an open codex.

Petrarch, as has been indicated, created a new ideal for private libraries which remained a model down to the time of Machiavelli and indeed has not yet lost its influence;[3] at the same time, stimulated by a knowledge of ancient libraries, he also conceived the plan of founding a large public institution. In 1362 he bestowed his own book collection upon the Bascilica of Saint Mark in Venice "for the comfort of the intelligent and noble people who may happen to take delight in such things,"[4] and in so doing expressed the wish that the Venetian government might provide for its care and growth in such a way that it would become the equal of ancient libraries. Of course this plan was not carried out, but it did point the way for posterity. Boccaccio looked up to Petrarch as to his teacher and master. Under Petrarch's influence he became a tireless and successful hunter of manuscripts. With the exaggeration typical also of the later Humanists, he tells us that on a visit to Monte Cassino he found the venerable library there in a state of unbelievable neglect. Similar enthusiasm was developed by the Chancellor of Florence, Salutati, a man younger by about twenty years. He was already searching—as many other scholars did in the following century—for a Livy manuscript supposed to be hidden somewhere in the far North. In this period bibliophily was already assuming occasional grotesque forms which subjected it to public scorn. In general, however, we must point out that during the whole fourteenth century these new ideas and aspirations affected only a few leading figures; it was not until the fifteenth century that they were appropriated by wider circles. What had formerly passed for a program now became fact.

The most important center of the great scholarly achievements which we owe to the fifteenth century was the Florence of Cosimo de Medici. We cannot say that he brought into being a court of the Muses on the banks of the Arno, but we can point to him as its patron in the noblest sense of the word. His literary minister was Niccoli, known for his treatise on orthography and his efforts in behalf of the new Renaissance script, and famous above all for his thoroughly systematic manuscript collecting. He raised the number of volumes in his own library to 800; and as often as his money gave out, Cosimo was obliged to come to the rescue. A modern historian aptly calls Niccoli "the 'trade list'[5] for all announcements concerning libraries and books." He sent his agents everywhere seeking out classic authors, and in this enterprise he exploited heavily the foreign trading system of the Medici. One of his instructions giving directions for thoroughly searching German monasteries has survived.

No one carried out Niccoli's commissions with greater zeal than Poggio. From the Council of Constance, to which he went as papal secretary, he visited German and French monasteries, especially St. Gall and Cluny. In the customary manner he uttered bitter complaints about the state of the libraries in these places and declared it his duty to free the treasures of antiquity from their bonds. When he could do nothing else, he copied texts, but he preferred to "save" them by thrusting them under his robe. Anyone who wishes to get a good, although historically not altogether accurate, picture of his activities should read C.F. Meyer's fine story "Plautus im Nonnenkloster."[6] It must be emphasized at this point that Poggio and his colleagues brought together the principal part of the Latin classics upon which later generations subsisted.

Just as important was the second act of the Humanistic enterprise—procuring the monuments of Greek literature at the collapse of the Byzantine Empire. At first refugees from the East brought manuscripts with them; then the Italians themselves, impelled by thirst for knowledge and love of adventure, hurried there to fetch them back. Just like Poggio in the North, Aurispa was at work here in the first decades of the fifteenth century, and he reports of himself: "I remember having given up my clothes to the Greeks in Constantinople in order to get codices—

Figure 22: Poggio, from a woodcut by N. Reusner.

something for which I feel neither shame nor regret."[7] Many Venetian nobles, e.g. the Giustiniani, took a lively interest in these discoveries, as the city of canals, primarily because of its relations with the Orient, was the natural starting-point for such expeditions and quickly developed into a center for trade in Greek manuscripts.

During the entire fifteenth century this enthusiasm for collecting did not abate: it lasted until the time of Lorenzo de Medici and Poliziano. Toward the end of the century the rediscovery of the old codices at Bobbio caused a particular sensation, and, as one Italian has said, with this event "the heroic age of discovery came to an end," (*si chiude l'età eroica delle scoperte*).[8] The full value of these accumulated treasures was intensively explored, and during the entire fifteenth century there quickly ripened a powerful impetus to philological and historical research in which a whole flock of Humanists took part, among them leading thinkers like Bruni, Valla, and Biondo.

At this time, too, Petrarch's cherished project of founding a large public library, which after his death Salutati had again brought forward, became a reality. Niccoli designated 1430 manuscripts which he left behind to the public "for the common use of all," (*in publico a commune utilità di ognuno*), and Cosimo provided for them a worthy dwelling in the monastery of Saint Mark, which he himself had had erected. He also gave liberally to other religious institutions, but did not as a consequence forget his own private library. Out of such beginnings developed the later Laurentian Library, (Biblioteca Mediceo-Laurenziana) which was fostered and enriched most of all by his grandson, Lorenzo. This scion of the Medici was aided first by the already-mentioned Poliziano and later by the Greek Lascaris, who undertook two separate journeys to the Orient in his employ.

Next to Venice, Florence was the great market for buying classic authors. In the Via degli Librai were housed the manuscript dealers with their employees. The most famous of these dealers was Vespasiano da Bisticci, whose shop served as a rendezvous for the literary world. He had broad bibliographical knowledge and assembled entire libraries from near and far for his noble customers. By using 45 scribes he once delivered on order to Cosimo 200 volumes in 22 months. Prices were not low, especially when classic works were dealt in. For this reason Bisticci exerted himself to get texts as correct as possible and took care that in matters of writing-material, script miniature-decoration and binding all the demands of Renaissance taste should be satisfied.

One of his best customers was the great bibliophile, Frederick of Montefeltro, Duke of Urbino. He appears to have spent as much as 30,000 ducats upon his collection and to have kept steadily occupied 30 to 40 copyists. Place was provided for the luxurious and splendidly ornamented manuscripts in rooms specially set aside for this purpose in his newly erected castle. Frederick endeavored to achieve in his library the highest possible completeness, embracing all branches of knowledge, and he had catalogues brought from foreign libraries, even that of Oxford, in order to determine possible gaps. That the library was intended for study is shown not only by the plan of the hall, which took into consideration the most favorable lighting conditions, but also by written directions for the librarian which have come down to us. Of him it is required that he be "learned, of good appearance, good natured, proficient in both literary and common language,"[9] that he keep good order, prepare catalogues, protect his books from every injury yet make them easily and conveniently accessible to those interested, and finally, that he keep a careful record of all borrowing.

To Bisticci at Florence also came orders from foreign lands, for example, from Mattias Corvinus, King of Hungary. Married to a Neapolitan princess, Corvinus strenghtened the ties already in existence between his country and Italy. He drew to his court Italian scholars and men of letters, artists and craftsmen, in order, as contemporaries said in praising him after his death, "to make Hungary another Italy" (*Pannoniam alteram Italiam reddere*). For this reason his large library furnished surpassing proof of the productivity of contemporary Italy in things scholarly as well as artistic. After Corvinus's death in 1490 the collection at Buda was scattered to the four winds, so that today they are found among the treasures of very many European libraries.[10]

Just as at Florence and Urbino, distinguished libraries came into being in the fifteenth century at the courts of many Italian nobles: Naples, Pavia, Ferrara, and Venice being examples. The Aragon rulers of Naples were among the most exalted patrons of the new culture and hence took a decidedly personal interest in their books. It was different with the Visconti and the Sforza, who, to be sure, busily added to the library at Pavia, partly from the spoils of war, but considered it in the main as an ornament of their court. The Ferrara library displayed quite an individual character. The Este family ruling there still devoted themselves to the courtly manners of chivalry along with Renaissance culture. This was shown in the composition of their library, which even had a group of French manuscripts. Finally, so far as the Library of St. Mark (Biblioteca Marciana) in Venice is concerned, it was the creation of the Greek Bessarion, who rose to the rank of cardinal and became a focus of Renaissance civilization. In 1468 he bequeathed his important collection, consisting principally of Greek manuscripts, to the city of canals as "the natural link between Orient and Occident." The Library of St. Mark was made available at once in liberal manner to the public, but it was not until the fifth decade of the following century that it acquired a worthy home in the splendid edifice designed by Sansovino.

There still remains to be considered the largest and most important library of the fifteenth century—the Vatican. What had formerly been assembled as a result of the collectors' enthusiasm of the Avignon popes, was lost during the great schism. Returned to Rome, the pontiffs had to begin again right from the start. About 1432 a Humanist reported after a visit to the Vatican Library: "I found nothing whatsoever worth remembering" *(nihil omino memoria dignum inveni).* Thus Nicholas V (1447-1455) really founded the papal collection anew. As a humble priest he already experienced "a certain inexplicable thirst for books" *(certe inesplicabile sete di libri),* and he especially searched for Greek manuscripts, often plunging himself thereby deep into debt. Like his friend Bisticci, he developed into an outstanding expert on matters pertaining to books and libraries. Because of this, Cosimo entrusted him with drawing up a canon which should contain the works necessary to a library worthy of respect, and which also, tradition has it, served as a model in the establishment of the library of Urbino and many another.[11]

In the person of Nicholas, therefore, the greatest bibliophile among the popes ascended the throne at Rome. He took over from his predecessors about 350 manuscripts: to this was added his own private library. After the jubilee year of 1450 had brought in very large sums of money, he sent agents everywhere, even to Scandinavia and the distant Orient, to track down classical authors. Assisted by his librarian, Tortelli, he planned a complete translation of Greek literature into Latin, and to this end gathered about him a whole swarm of scholars and copyists. Rome was once again to become the center of the scholarly and literary world. Part of the grand building program which

Figure 23: Pope Nicholas V, founder of the Vatican Library.

aimed at the reorganization on a monumental scale of the Leonine quarter was a library "large and ample for the general convenience of learned men" *(ingens et ampla pro communi doctorum virorum commodo).* In this way, Nicholas hoped, his name would be honored with those of Ptolemy and Trajan. Early death brought many of his projects to an untimely end. Despite this, about 800 Latin and over 400 Greek manuscripts had been brought together. With these the Vatican was already moving into first place among the libraries of Italy.

Sixtus IV (1471-1484) continued the work of Nicholas and in some measure finished it, not so much by setting to work personally as by making available the necessary money and by selecting an excellent librarian, the Humanist Platina. The number of

Figure 24: The Vatican Library, 18th century watercolor.

Figure 25: Hall of Sixtus V, Vatican Library.

volumes mounted to over 3500, and now rooms worthy of them were provided, with decorations by the ranking artists of the time. The quarters were divided into Latin and Greek sections, and a reserve library set aside for the protection of rarities. Platina took care of everything—arrangement, classification, cataloguing. The library was open to the public and there were no difficulties about lending books, as journals which have survived testify. Ariosto could say with justice: "Sixtus had ancient books gathered from all over the world for public use."[12]

The principle that libraries should be open to the public may well serve as one characteristic differentiating the Renaissance library from the library of the Middle Ages. Were there, however, other fundamental differences between the two? The answer is in part affirmative, in part negative: what had disappeared was the specifically medieval atmosphere. The Humanists and literary men who banded together into academies at the courts of various noblemen in the manner of the ancient world looked upon the library in the old sense of a place for exchange of scholarly ideas and for esthetic enjoyment. Still dominant among them was a burning desire for the uncorrupted sources of Greek and Roman literature—a desire which Petrarch had aroused in former times, only now the enthusiasm of the fourteenth century had given way to a quieter and clearer objectivity. Because of this desire, however, medieval authors were not barred from library shelves.

In the library of Nicholas V, classical and Humanistic, Scholastic and patristic works stood peacefully side by side. This was true not only of the Vatican Library, which was primarily the collection of the Pope, but likewise of other large institutions. Indeed this universal character of the Middle Ages even found expression in paintings which decorated the walls of these buildings. Like the artists of the late Middle Ages, Melozzo da Forli chose allegories representing the liberal arts and the faculties of instruction in the universities as subjects for his frescoes in the halls of Urbino. Raphael himself adorned the private library of Julius II, the renowned Stanza della Segnatura, with such a "pictorial representation of a book catalogue."[13]

As for the individual volumes in the Renaissance library, they show a good deal of variation from medieval manuscripts. It has already been pointed out above how a Bisticci took contemporary taste into account in the whole make-up of the book. Shelving and classification, on the other hand, had remained the same. There was no pressing reason for a change in the system. Although the number of books had increased through the influx of classic and Humanist authors, this by no means made it impossible to handle them in the same old way. The products of the printing presses were, on the whole, rigidly excluded by bibliophiles such as Montefeltro. Only with the end of the century did they begin gradually to penetrate. This is what the sources say concerning the desks in the Library of Saint Mark in Florence; this is what we find in a painting of the Vatican Library; and printed books as well as chained codices have been preserved unharmed in the beautiful early Renaissance room at Cesena which Malatesta Novello had erected in 1452. Even the Laurentian Library, built from the plans of Michelangelo, stuck to the old usage.

The library at Zutphen, which, like that at Cesna, has kept its original aspect unchanged, serves to illustrate the fact that north of the Alps, too, during this entire period, the medieval system of arranging books was dominant. And why, indeed, should it be otherwise? At this time Italy led all the rest in library development, while England, France and Germany merely followed the trails she blazed.

The England of the Wars of the Roses showed, in general, little inclination to devote itself to encouraging the new culture. The bonds which Chaucer had already forged between his native land and Italy did not strengthen.[14] An exception to this rule was Humphrey, Duke of Gloucester, son of Henry IV, who was unusual in another respect also. He avidly studied the classical writers, borrowed books from Italian Humanists, and permitted them to dedicate their works to him. His truly comprehensive collections passed by gift into the possession of the Oxford University Library, and this led to the building of Duke Humphrey's Library in 1488.

France too still retained its medieval culture through the fifteenth century. Epoch-making here were the two Italian campaigns of Charles VIII and Louis XII. The former brought back to Paris in 1495 parts of the Aragon library of Naples, while five years later Louis carried off as spoils of war the Sforza library of Pavia. This made its way to the castle of Blois, which the king had already in earlier days fitted out plentifully with book-treasures. At this time there were already among the high French nobility Renaissance bibliophiles, of whom the most brilliant representative was Louis' minister, Cardinal d'Amboise. He showed a special preference for Italian manuscripts, and acquired by purchase another part of the Aragon legacy. But the new spirit first began truly to expand under Francis I. He had the Blois collections removed to his favorite seat at Fontainebleau and built there a library which compares favorably with its Italian models in every respect. As *maitre de la librairie* the king appointed the great philologist and jurist Budé; furthermore we find there with him Lascaris, whom we have met before in Florence and who now looked after Greek manuscripts for Francis as he had done formerly for the Medici. Quite in the Italian manner the library was made accessible to all those interested; in fact, Francis personally subsidized the editing of valuable texts.

From the time of Charles VIII the library contained printed books, though for a long while these continued to remain in the background as over against manuscripts.

Figure 26: Four scenes from the Royal Library, 1488–89. From an illuminated manuscript, "La mer des histoires."

Of great importance, however, was the introduction of legal deposit by the French king. As recent investigations have shown, this arrangement developed in connection with the machinery of book-censorship and the conferring of the privilege of printing books, in that both were used as means of forcing the donation of free copies to the kings for their libraries. This was effected by laws of Francis I in 1537-1538. Later on in our story we shall see how other rulers followed his example and how today copyright forms one of the most important sources of growth for all large public libraries.

The influence of the Italian Quattrocento upon Germany was stronger and more lasting than upon England and France.[15] With the reform councils of Constance and Basel the new tendencies forced their way across the Alps. Among the pioneers were the above-mentioned manuscript-hunters, chief among them the important personage of Aeneus Silvius Piccolomini (later Pius II). The German Humanism which developed did not for a long time hence involve any break with the medieval point of view or any turning away from Scholasticism.

Its primary effort was toward better formal education and more exact knowledge of the literary sources of classical antiquity. Only gradually did a more aggressive attitude set in. More vigorously than in other lands the German middle classes took part in the spreading of Humanism, linking it directly to the educational efforts we have just mentioned above.

The Humanistic doctrines also had a strong effect upon German library affairs. The improvement described in the preceding chapter, especially in the cities, proceeded as before, but with the difference that within the book collection the percentage of ancient, and later also of Italian, books slowly and gradually increased. One of the first to open his library to the new culture was Nicholas of Cusa (d. 1464), the great prince of the Church and original scholar, who competed with the Italians in collecting classical manuscripts. Of his followers I shall

Figure 27: A bibliophile at his reading desk, 15th century woodcut.

name the Augsburg patrician, Gossembrot, and the Frankish baron, Albrecht von Eyb. In the aldermen's library and the church libraries of Nuremberg one can observe how since the eighties classical and Humanistic literature had been gaining strength. About this time Philip, Count Palatine of the Rhine, modeled his court at Heidelberg completely on the Italian style and maintained intellectual contacts with men such as Von Dalberg, Agricola, and others of like disposition. The Palatine library took on a strongly Humanistic coloring, while the library of Heidelberg University—and this is true also of its sister universities—preserved the traditions of the Middle Ages down to the next century.

The middle-class character of German Humanism is shown by the pains taken to make Latin and Italian literature available to wider classes of people by means of translation. Nikolas von Wyle, town clerk of Esslingen, had a special enthusiasm for these translations. Very near him lived the Princess Palatine Mechthild, who built herself a library on her dowager's estate at Rottemberg on the Neckar and there busily collected older German literature.

In the meantime Gutenberg's discovery had been spread far and wide by German printers. Around the turn of the century there already flourished a lively book trade covering almost the whole of western Europe. Its most active spot was Basel, where at the time the leader of northern Humanism, Erasmus, held court—we might almost say—and gathered the Basel Group (*sodalitas Basiliensis*) about him. Within their ranks there developed an intensive cooperation between scholarship and printing: while the Humanists functioned as editors, the followers of Gutenberg, above all Froben, "the prince of German printers," took care of the publishing of classic and Humanistic works. From Basel commercial and intellectual lines of connection ran to Lyons, the chief printing city of western Europe, as well as to Venice, where Aldus Manutius had his workshop. In Basel lived also the philologist Sichardus, about whose regular visits to old monasteries in order to find basic materials fit for his editions we have detailed knowledge.

We are most interested, however, in the consequences of printing for the development of libraries. A two-fold effect can be stated. Up to this period, as we have tried to show, libraries and *scriptoria* had at all times been closely bound to one another. One need only recall the pagan academies and the Christian monasteries, or the bibliophiles of ancient times, of the Middle Ages, and again of the Italian Renaissance. In the course of the sixteenth century this close connection between the makers and the collectors of books was dissolved forever. This was one effect of the 'black art'; the other, the sharp increase in book production and the emergence of a host of hitherto unsuspected library problems in connection with it, was yet to make itself felt in the course

Figure 28: A printing house. Engraving by A. von Verdt.

Figure 29: A printing house. Engraving by Hans merian, 17th century.

of time. The first thing to change was the arrangement of the books, in that, as we have already observed in Italy and France, the printed book now took its place alongside the manuscript.

This held true, for example, of the library of the Nuremberg Humanist and polyhistor, Hartmann Schedel (d. 1514). Part of his collection derived from the estate of his cousin Hermann, the rest from trips to Italy or visits to German monasteries. Many of the texts had been copied in his own hand. But among nearly 600 items shown in the catalogue, up to a third were printed books. Schedel loved to decorate his books with maxims and little illustrations and to inscribe in them biographical sketches of the authors. His famous compatriot, Pirkheimer, belonged to a younger generation. Well educated and highly cultured, he embodied in his person the Italian ideal of the well-rounded man, though with German middle-class nuances. The way in which he managed his costly library, which contained among other things the complete set of Aldine Greek imprints, is revealed by the motto of his bookplate: For himself and his friends (*Sibi et amicis*). What Pirkheimer was to Nuremberg, Peutinger was to Augsburg. His library was held in high esteem by all the Humanists. It was well classified and catalogued and comprised over 2100 volumes—among them, however, only 170 manuscripts.

Both Pirkheimer and Peutinger were among the closest friends of Maximilian I, who rose to be the intellectual center of German Humanism and most enthusiastically promoted the art of printing. It is not correct, however, to attribute to this ruler the founding of the Court Library at Vienna. The books he collected as prince, along with those he inherited from his father, and whatever was added later, Maximilian kept partly at Wiener-Neustadt, partly at Innsbruck, and partly at other castles. Ferdinand I seems to have laid the real foundation for the Vienna library.

A whole series of important Humanist libraries could still be cited. The collector of books had now become so popular a figure in Germany that the satirist Brant included him among his types of fools. Let us point out then only Reuchlin's library, rich in Greek and Hebrew texts, the library of Beatus Rhenanus in Schlettstadt, well preserved even to this day, and finally the library at Sponheim, which the abbot Tritheim founded. Tritheim has been compared with Cassiodorus, because like him he endeavored to rescue the treasures of the past for posterity. Yet he stood at the end of a movement, while the earlier man had stood at the beginning of one. Cassiodorus, as was shown earlier, successfully bridged the gap between ancient and medieval times, and created at Vivarium the model for western monastic libraries. Tritheim, on the contrary, made the vain attempt to implant Humanism at Sponheim. The books which he had assembled there with great effort and industry were quickly scattered again by his successors. Indeed the hour was not far distant when Sponheim, like so many another monastic library throughout the length and breadth of Germany, was to vanish completely.

Chapter VI.

The Reformation And The Seventeenth Century

The Reformation forms an epoch in the history of libraries. In this period many a medieval library ceased to exist while a large number of new libraries had their origin. Not infrequently, at the dissolution of German monasteries and religious institutions, the acquisitions resulting from many centuries of zealous collecting were carelessly disposed of or destroyed as papist literature. Revolutionary movements like the Peasants' War of 1524-25 wrought the worst havoc. From Thuringia down the Main, through the Odenwald and the Black Forest to Switzerland, ecclesiastical libraries had heavy losses to bemoan; many, such as that at Reinhardsbrunn, met total destruction. The same thing happened also outside Germany, for example in France during the Huguenot Wars. In 1562, to cite just one instance, Condé's soldiers plundered the treasures of Fleury-sur-Loire. Things seem to have gone worst in England. During the thirty years in which about 800 monasteries and convents were secularized, their book collections received the most careless treatment. In 1550 the Commissioners of Edward VI even came to Oxford and so completely emptied the library that shortly thereafter the furniture of the room as sold as useless.

If we should not pass over in silence the destructive effect of the Reformation, there is all the more reason to emphasize vigorously its constructive influence. In the circular letter of Luther in 1524 "To the Mayors and Aldermen of all the cities of Germany"[1] occurs this significant sentence: "Finally, this must also be taken into consideration...that no cost nor pains should be spared to procure good libraries in suitable buildings, especially in the large cities, which are able to afford it." Melancthon,

"Germany's teacher" (*praeceptor Germaniae*), also worked with the same purpose. It can easily be observed in various regions that this was not merely a matter of words and exhortations, but that deeds followed words. One need only recall in this respect the beneficent activity which John Bugenhagen carried on over all northern Germany. In this activity the book collections formerly belonging to Catholic institutions generally furnished the chief materials for the institutions about to be founded.

In this way, alongside the municipal libraries dating from the fifteenth century, there arose many new ones, as in Hamburg, Nuremberg, and Augsburg, to say nothing of church libraries which served substantially the same ends, as in Bremen and Halle. In many places a collection simply passed from Catholic to Protestant hands without the slightest alterations. To these were added the many new school libraries, among which, once again, those in Saxony stood out notably. The universities founded at this time, Königsberg, Helmstedt, Jena and Marburg—we should perhaps add Leyden— acquired their needed book stock in the same way; those already in existence, e.g. Leipzig, now came to possess true university libraries. In the Catholic regions the re-establishment of libraries set in as the counter-Reformation gathered strength. In this work the Jesuits, particularly Canisius, performed lasting services which unfortunately have to this day failed to receive any comprehensive evaluation in the literature on the subject.[2]

All these passed for public libraries, but in no way did they possess the arrangements to which we are accustomed in such institutions. Access was, as a rule, restricted to a privileged group. Administration and internal organization still left almost everything to be desired. The growth of the collection was left largely to chance, and depended upon the good will of liberal donors. Of course, Gutenberg's invention made its influence felt and caused the number of books in libraries to increase from decade to decade. But realization of the new duties which devolved upon libraries as a result of this invention seemed to have dawned quite gradually. Furthermore, the need of the time for usable public institutions was materially undermined by the great abundance of private collections.

In a Meissen chronicle we read: "It is quite common for most of the nobles and burghers, even if they do not actually study, to be able to at least to read and write, to bring together in their homes fine libraries of all sorts of good books of godly writings and to attract to their hearths excellent and profitable historians, physicians, and others." We may take it that among the urban patricians the number of learned bibliophiles had risen since the previous period. Two of them, members of the Fugger family, will concern us farther on. Even among artisans the joys of book collecting had spread to such an extent that Hans Sachs, with his grand collection of semi-scientific works, seems not to have been altogether an unusual phenomenon. Tradition has handed down the names of certain noble families whose libraries encompassed several thousand volumes. It can clearly be seen how movements proceeding from Humanism combined with interest in contemporary religious questions to cause large classes of the people to occupy themselves with books.

Also, in the sixteenth century many territorial princes studied at some university and continued their scholarly contacts during their reigns. Along with fitting out a library, they aimed at the same time to enhance the splendor of their courts and to provide the necessary book materials for officials with their ever-increasing administrative duties. Naturally, at times private interests prevailed and at times motives of state. At any rate, at this very time there arose a group of libraries which today are reckoned among the most important in Germany.

For example, in the thirties Duke Albert of Prussia set up in his castle at Königsberg both a public and also a private library, and Julius of Brunswick in 1568 laid the foundations of the famous collection at Wolfenbüttel. The founding of the Dresden library by August of Saxony had occurred somewhat earlier, and a little later there came the founding of the library of Cassel by William of Hesse. Since the printing of books was now done only on a mass-production basis, so to speak, bindings alone now afforded the possibility of satisfying the individual's desire for luxury. The bounds to which this display of ostentation would go are shown by the oft-mentioned Silver Library of Königsberg.[3] As a rule, however, a leather binding with blind tooling and gilding was favored, the finest examples of which were produced by the Wittenberg bookbinders and by the Heidelberg craftsmen employed by Ott Heinrich.

Of this Elector Palatine a poet sang: "At all times he loved wisdom and art."[4] Among his most intimate friends was the distinguished Grecist and brilliant bibliophile, Ulrich Fugger. Ott Heinrich's predecessors had already brought together considerable collections of books; he enlarged them with unflagging zeal to the time of his death (1559)—to this, the ancient monasteries along the Rhine, especially Lorsch, can bear witness. Ott Heinrich specialized in German manuscripts. His successors made further acquisitions, such as Ulrich Fugger's library, and took eager advantage of the Frankfurt book fairs. Extraordinarily liberal access was provided to this library, and valuable codices were often turned over to scholars for editing. In this way, until the catastrophe of 1623, the Palatine Library ranked as the most outstanding of German libraries and played the role of a kind of intellectual center for the whole Southwest.

The founding and support of libraries was by no means confined to Protestant princes, however. Proof of this is the Vienna Court Library, which at the end of the century had 9000 volumes, including 1600 manuscripts, and was administered by the able Blotius. The best proof is the work of Duke Albert V of Bavaria. Unlike his cousin the elector, Albert had no close association with art and knowledge: he loved ostentation and, as was later said of him, in collecting books he desired to imitate other rulers in this method of developing a splendid court. Consequently, true credit for the founding of the Munich library belongs to that John Jacob Fugger whom the Italians called "the richest and most learned man in Germany: (*il primo ricco e'l piu dotto di Germania*). He made use of the widespread ramifications of his family's business enterprises to secure for himself, especially, Greek manuscripts and he also bought the library of Schedel, already familiar to us. First of all he induced Albert in 1558 to buy the valuable collections of the statesman and Orientalist, Widmanstetter. Somewhat later his own books came into the Duke's possession. The approximately 11,000 volumes so assembled were brought together in a new annex to the duke's residence. In the years that followed, the collection was much enlarged, especially under Maximilian I, who himself drew up instructions for administering the library and in 1602 had the catalogue of Greek manuscripts published. Later a law was promulgated by his son favoring the Munich library with the copyright deposit of all printed books, a privilege which the Vienna library had already enjoyed for quite some time.

In Duke Albert we can observe for the first time that liking for luxury and show, that partiality for the costly and rare, which had started up among the aristocracy at the height of the Renaissance and which grew more and more to be an essential characteristic of succeeding generations. Before long every fashionable prince's court had a cabinet or art objects connected with the library as well as its cabinet of rarities. A rule of the year 1635 for "museums or libraries" (*musei sive bibliothecae*) held as desirable in the great hall of the library the bringing together of "some of the things which the native curiosity of a learned man is wont to delight in as food befitting, so to speak, the liberal mind, such as mathematical instruments, ancient coins, learned fragments of former times, as well as certain miracles of nature and art."[5]

What we have set forth up to this point can well be summarized in the statement that Germany in the sixteenth century was saturated with books. At this time the focus of the international book trade was also situated in Germany, and the catalogue of the Frankfurt book fair (*Frankfurter Messkatalog*) furnished the most complete survey of European literature. Finally, it was a German, the physician and universal scholar, Conrad Gesner, who in 1545 founded scientific bibliography with his *Biblioteca universalis*.[6] Nevertheless it was denied to Germany to keep this leadership. General decline and decay, then the frightful catastrophe of the Thirty Years' War, caused Germany to be displaced by the other great powers of the West. It is clear, then, that the largest and most important collections of the seventeenth century are to be looked for outside Germany and also that in these other lands the new type, which we may refer to as the baroque library, took shape.

In the foregoing chapter it was pointed out how the Renaissance stuck to the medieval plan of arranging books, still preferring to keep them lying chained on desks. However, the more the productivity of printing presses increased and thereby the number of books in libraries mounted, the more the inadequacies of this earlier method must have made themselves felt. Relief came first through a new device: the books were placed in rows in bookcases which ran along the walls. Soon, when it became necessary to extend the cases to the ceiling, an important advance was made by introducing galleries which made possible access to the upper shelves. Still, practical needs alone did not bring about this innovation; it expressed also the dictates of contemporary taste. As the central space was left free of books, the opportunity arose to exhibit curiosa and rarities. In this way the library took on more and more the character of a baroque exhibition room.

So far as is now known, Philip II's great architect, Herrera, was one of the first to carry out consistently the placing of books in wall cases. The years from 1563 to 1584 saw the building of the majestically dark Escorial, in which the king himself lived like a scholarly monk. Under his personal supervision the library grew extraordinarily fast, by far its greatest riches coming as a legacy of the statesman De Mendoza. The librarian Montano followed unusual principles in classification: first he divided the collection by language, then

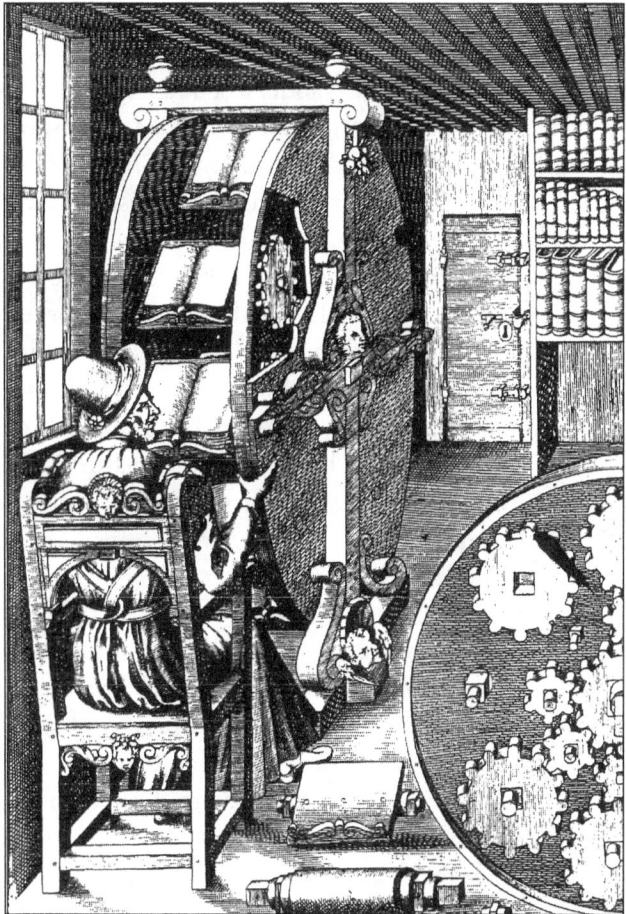

Figure 30: "The Book Wheel" by A. Ramelli, 16th century.

separated manuscripts and printed books, and finally divided everything into 64 separate subject classes.

In France the Royal Library did not suffer neglect under the successors of Francis I. These rulers indulged in singular luxury in bindings; and, thanks to the high perfection of bookmaking in France, the king's binders (*relieurs du roi*) were capable of satisfying the most pretentious requirements. The stock of valuable manuscripts grew first through the collection of Catherine de Medici, then through that of Cardinal d'Amboise, of which we have already spoken. An important step was the transfer of the library from Fontainebleau to Paris. There it was under the direction of the librarian Rigault, who completed its first catalogue in 1622.

But despite internal and external progress the Biblioteque du Roi was soon put completely in the shade by the library which Cardinal Mazarin fashioned. This powerful statesman interested himself no more than was customary in science and art, but at his side stood Gabriel Naudé, a scholar of rank and the *beau ideal* of library directors. His *Avis pour dresser une bibliothèque*,[7] published in 1627, set out a program for a universal library, provided with the most important books in all branches of knowledge in their original languages and in translation, along with the best commentaries and reference works. Naudé fought the prevailing partiality for rarities, desired equal consideration for older as well as more recent literature, and even wished to procure heretical writings. An unclassified collection seemed to him to deserve the name of library as little as a crowd of men deserve to be called an army. As the best classification he recommended that which is "easiest and most natural" (*la plus facile, la plus naturelle*), which was built upon the faculties and contained reasonable subdivisions. All these proposals were based upon the same idea, namely, that such a collection should not only promote the fame of its owner but should at the same time satisfy the needs of the public.

After Naudé had entered Mazarin's service in 1642, he found the opportunity to effect his program. Gifts streamed in from all sides. Generals and diplomats abroad were given commissions to carry out. Naudé himself undertook long journeys to England, Flanders, Germany, and Italy. Ultimately, some 40,000 books were brought together, all luxuriously bound in morocco and stamped in gold with the Cardinal's coat of arms. And while the Bibliothèque du Roi still kept its doors shut, Mazarin dedicated his library "to all those who desired to come there to study" (à tous ceux *qui y vouloient aller estudier*). But this most excellent and beautiful library, this eighth wonder of the world, as Naudé called it, fell prey to the Fronde at the opening of the fifties. Its seizure called forth from Naudé a cry of anguish, for he loved his handiwork as a father loves his only child.[8] But when his plea to the *parlement*, as passionate as it was proud, fell upon deaf ears, he left the place where he had accomplished so much and sought service in foreign lands. Mazarin, as we know, later returned to power and began forthwith the restoration of his library, but death overtook his librarian on the way back.

In order to understand the approach and the achievement of Naudé we must keep in mind the fact that his life coincided with the new growth of knowledge represented by such names as Scaliger and De Thou, Grotius and Hobbes, Galileo and Kepler, Bacon and Descartes. In such a period, as is easy to understand, there arose among all those who did not merely collect books, but studied them too, a desire to provide for systematic organization and expert administration of collections of books running not to hundreds but to thousands and tens of thousands. Consequently at this time the vocation of a librarian with practical training took on heightened importance, which mounted even higher during the following centuries. That in the case in point an extremely gifted representative of this profession should meet up with the most liberal of patrons was a fortunate twist of fate. Yet Naudé could already be guided by excellent examples; he himself named the Bodleian and the Ambrosian Library.

The first of these was the magnanimous work of Sir Thomas Bodley, a typical representative of Elizabethan England, in whom the common sense of the practical man was combined with a good Humanistic training. He had studied and taught at Oxford and had later come to know several courts on the continent through diplomatic service. He believed, as his autobiography reveals, that in the twilight of his life he could perform no better service than "to set up my staff at the library door" in Oxford with the purpose of restoring the university library which had been destroyed decades before, and putting it again to public use. He believed that he possessed the necessary equipment—scholarly attainments, sufficient funds, distinguished friends, and undisturbed leisure. And so, in 1598, Bodley made his offer to the vice-Chancellor of the university and after five years of labor, during which he spared neither money nor energy, and also found the readiest support from all sides, the library was able to open in its old quarters.

It was justly called the Bodleian, for the enthusiasm of its founder never abated. He induced the Stationers' Company of London to give it free copies of all new books, and he willed his own property to the university. In accordance with the statute drawn up by Bodley, the library was open five hours each day; only graduates, however, had free access. The books were arranged in classes without subdivisions. The first printed catalogue appeared as early as 1605; the second, in 1620 testified to the great growth of the collection. In a very short time the old building proved too small. In Bodley's own lifetime a small wing was built, and in the year of his death (1613) work was begun on

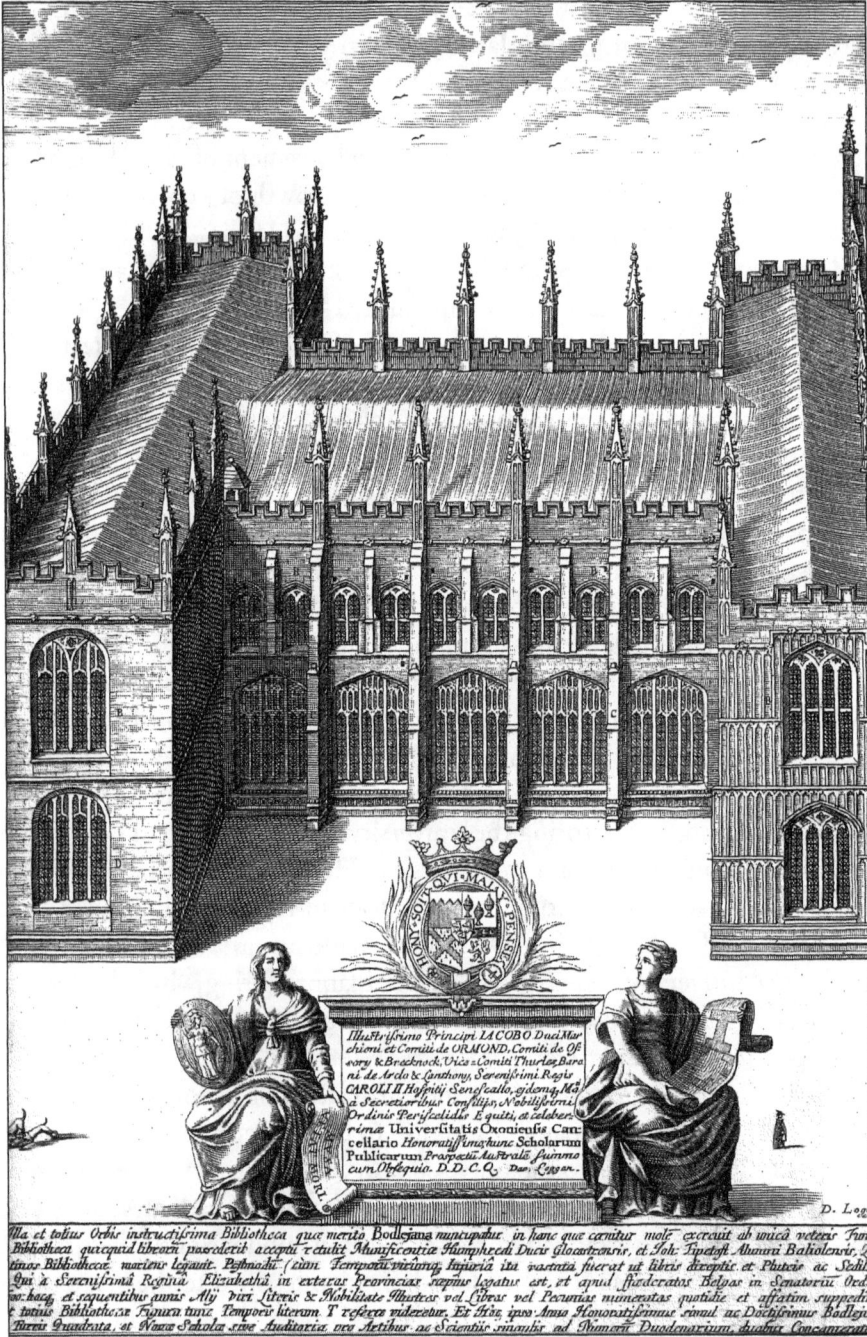

Figure 31: The Bodleian Library, by David Loggan.

one considerably larger.[9] These additions had galleries with steps which led to the upper rows of bookshelves. The same system had already been installed a few years earlier in the Ambrosian Library. This library may in general be pointed to as the Catholic counterpart of Bodley's creation.

Manzoni, in *The Betrothed (I Promessi Sposi)*, has drawn us a picture of the Archbishop of Milan, Federigo Borromeo. The Archbishop followed squarely in the footsteps of his great kinsman and predecessor, Carlo. Himself an able scholar and prolific author, he strove to establish the new Catholic scholarship on a firm foundation. The founding of his library also served this purpose. Since it was to be not merely a collection of minds long dead, but rather a living center of work, he placed it under the direction of a College of Doctors, for whose own publications a special printing press was set up. To this was added an Academy of Arts with rich art collections. And to house everything a special building was erected in the years 1603-09. The Ambrosian Library contained many thousands of books and manuscripts, among them valuable treasures from the monastery of Bobbio, and it excelled in Orientalia. It was decided that it "should be open to all for study" (*omnibus studiorum causa pateat*).

Similar liberality prevailed at Rome in the Angelica, which the Augustinian Rocca founded in the first decade of the seventeenth century. It ruled no less at the Vatican Library just as it had as early as the Renaissance, though this was in sharp contrast to later practice. So Montaigne reports: "I saw the library without any difficulty; anybody sees it thus, and makes what extracts he pleases."[10] But Montaigne did not know the splendid new building which Sixtus V (1585-90) had built by Fontana. The Vatican Library in this period was also fortunate in having a good administration. Among its directors was the well-known church historian, Baronius, and its valuable manuscript catalogues were prepared by the brothers Rainaldi.

The seventeenth century brought to the Vatican Library a whole series of splendid gains, of which only the three most important can be mentioned. In 1658 the Library of Urbino, which, as we know, Frederick of Montefeltro had founded, passed into the papal possession. Approximately thirty years later the books from the estate of Christina of Sweden were purchased. This learned and remarkable woman, to whom Ranke devotes a special section in his history of the Popes, succeeding her father, Gustavus Adolfus, had most enthusiastically collected books and manuscripts and had not desisted during the whole of her unsettled life. Upon her removal to Rome she took along all her treasures. But the greatest sensation in the learned world was caused by the acquisition of the Palatine Library. After the capture of Heidelberg by Tilly's troops, Maximilian of Bavaria presented the library to the Pope in 1623, presumably for reasons essentially political. The transfer of this library to the Tiber was carried out with the greatest possible care and foresight. The old bindings, which had been detached before the transfer, were replaced by new bindings of fresh vellum. Each volume then received the inscription: "I am from that library which Maximilian, Duke of Bavaria, took as a prize of war from captured Heidelberg and sent as a trophy to Gregory XV."[11]

The Duke's actions have been subjected to many bitter reproaches. It does not befit the historian to join in the chorus of moral indignation. Library history teaches just this: that from Caesar to Napoleon—and beyond—libraries have been considered valuable prizes of war. It seems more dangerous to me to use the expropriation of the Palatine Library in confessional controversies, for the hero and saviour of Protestantism, Gustavus Adolfus, made ample use of the same practice on his widespread campaigns. Libraries everywhere were systematically emptied, the Jesuit colleges drawing special attention. This occurred in 1621 in the Baltic provinces and five years later in Prussia. In 1631 a similar fate befell Würzburg, Erfurt, Eichsfeld, Mainz, and the Rheingau; in the following years Breslau, Bamberg, and Munich. After the king's death the Swedish generals enthusiastically followed his example. In particular, libraries in Silesia, Bohemia, and Moravia fell prey to them. Gustavus Adolfus had had the rightfulness of his procedures established by legal opinions; he had also used the booty brought home essentially for ideal purposes. It appeared to him a means of raising the educational level of his country. Consequently books and manuscripts were distributed among different places in Sweden. The largest share, however, went to the University Library of Upsala, founded in 1621.

In all this Germany played the sufferer's role. For three decades the dogs of war raged through her provinces. Even if fortified cities suffered less harm than the open country, spiritual impoverishment engulfed all regions. The scattering and destruction of libraries was not the greatest evil: far worse was the widespread loss—by individual and society alike—of that contact with books which had distinguished Germany a century earlier. Now it was necessary to build and create anew. And here, as in other activities, the territorial princes were among the first to recognize the demands of the hour. The Wolfenbüttel library had been left by the grandson (Frederick Ulrich) of its founder, (Julius, Duke of Brunswick and Lüneburg) to the University of Helmstedt. Duke Augustus assembled on the old location a new and far more splendid library. He had received a careful education and as Prince, while the war raged outside, had lived in his "Ithaca," as he called it, only to collect and study books. Come to the throne in 1635, he busied himself conscientiously with the welfare of his domain. But his leisure hours belonged entirely to the Bibliotheca Augusta. Yearly he spent up to 16,000 thaler, so that at his death the library numbered some 28,000 volumes, including 2,000 manuscripts. With justifiable pride the Duke boasted: "Not only have we assembled our library with great care, expense, and exertion, but with manifold unbelievable labors we have brought it into such fine order and arrangement that the like is hardly to be found in all Europe." He was his own librarian and diligently wrote out the catalogues with his own hand. In classification he did not follow the scheme of classes and sub-classes recommended by Naudé, but separated the collection, as had been done at Oxford, into twenty coordinate classes.

Figure 32: Duke August in his library, 1650.

Motives other than those operating at Brunswick governed Ernest the Pious of Gotha (d. 1675). Dedicating all his powers to rebuilding the duchy, which had been devastated by war, he carried through a model administrative organization and labored so industriously in behalf of church and school that he was called the prince among pedagogues and the pedagogue among princes. Building the library represented only part of his educational program. The library consisted first of the older books, then of spoils of war which Ernest had brought home from his participation in Swedish campaigns; to these were added many purchases.

The library which Frederick William, the Great Elector, founded at Berlin, however, stands out as the finest example of royal solicitude. "Amid the roar of battle and the cavalcade of victories"[12] from Jutland in 1659 he gave the necessary orders to take

Figure 33: Herzog August Library.

the first steps. The opening of the library followed two years later, after the Peace of Oliva had made the possession of his domain secure. There were hardly any monastic treasures at hand to commandeer, and what former electors had bequeathed was also very insignificant. Nevertheless, by applying himself personally to the task, making sure that the library had a steady revenue, and inducing the presentation of valuable gifts, Frederick William brought the collection up to 20,000 printed books and 1,600 manuscripts. The director of the library was the Frankfurt professor, Hendreich. Though judgments of him differ, yet he did draw up catalogues and work out a classification which remained in use for over a hundred years. At first the library was located in a wing of the castle where it was at once made available to the public for use. Shortly before the death of the Elector a separate new building was begun, but this got only as far as the ground floor. Hendreich's eulogy extolled Frederick William's services in behalf of the library, and another scholar said in the magniloquent style of the time that he vied for honors with the rulers of Alexandria and Pergamum.

Chapter VII. The Enlightenment

"From the time of Leibniz to about the end of the eighteenth century there was in the realm of science, letters, and social life a uniform type of cultured individual in Europe and a *société anonyme* to which belonged the most diverse minds... This *société anonyme* no longer exists, but in libraries it lives on—and there it must continue to live."—Harnack in *Zentralblatt für Bibliothekswesen*, XL, p. 536.

In the period usually comprehended under the name of the Enlightenment the scientific progress which had set in during the preceding epoch pushed forward even more markedly. An optimistic urge toward research took hold, the like of which had been known only during the Renaissance. But men did not look back to the past as in that former time; on the contrary, they broke every bond of traditional authority. The autonomy of the mind working methodically was proclaimed, and men strove for rational explanation in all fields of knowledge. This new order of specialized research went hand in hand with a new systematization of the sciences, and with a new kind of organized international scholarly cooperation. In this period came the founding of most of the learned societies;[1] to this period western libraries owe their modern intellectual stamp.

We may begin our account with France, for in this age that country was not only typical of political and military power, but it also determined the style of living and held the lead in art and literature. Even if its scientific achievements were not always of first importance, it did lend the most elegant forms of expression to the intellectual productions of the time.

The second half of the seventeenth century, when Descartes was beginning to acquire followers and the skeptic Bayle was publishing his dictionary, also saw the birth of the truly scientific study of history in France. In publishing the *Acta Sanctorum*, the Jesuits set about systematically collecting and critically sifting source materials. A similar task was undertaken—with still better results—by the Benedictine Congregation of St. Maur, with the great scholar, Mabillon, at its head.[2] In Paris, at St. Germaindes-Prés, the Maurists created a kind of academy with a central library to which was brought the fullest possible collection of materials from the ancient monasteries of their order. After Mabillon came Montfaucon, who attempted a union catalogue of western manuscripts and is considered the father of the *catalogue raisonné*.

The scholarly endeavors of the Jesuits and Maurists came to have a special importance for French library history because of the lively interest which the great minister, Colbert, took in them. As bibliophile and collector he continued the tradition of Mazarin: his Naudé was the historian Baluze. Agents systematically toured the provinces for him, buying what was to be had, but also occasionally not hesitating to use somewhat objectionable methods. Yet the minister cared for the Royal Library, which had been placed under his direction in 1661, with equal enthusiasm. "Monsieur Colbert," said a contemporary, "forgets nothing that is necessary to augment and embellish the library in order to satisfy the generous inclination of his master."[3] French diplomats in foreign lands were called upon to buy books; special missions were sent to the Orient. For all this the necessary funds were forthcoming. And, since there was no lack of costly gifts, the library was able to quadruple its size by the time of the minister's death.

The upward trend which had begun for the library with Colbert persisted. Louis XIV supported it in every way, and his two successors on the throne did not lag behind his praiseworthy example. The whole court shared this enthusiasm for collecting, so that it was possible for one splendid private library after another to pass into the royal possession by gift or purchase. French diplomats abroad continued to be called upon frequently to perform services for the library, and scholars like the Maurists were charged with the acquisition of materials. Particularly rich was the influx of Orientalia from the Near East, and even from India and China. At the outset of the Revolution the Royal Library was rightly considered the largest and richest collection of books and manuscripts in the world.

Its internal organization kept pace with its enlargement. Of the officials involved, Clément deserves special mention, for, beginning in 1675, he undertook a re-arrangement of the collection into 23 classes, and for this purpose he completed the classed catalogue. Now also an inventory of the manuscripts was taken, a task in which the efforts of the Maurists and other scholars were enlisted once again. During this whole time the Bignon family contributed valuable services. Under the most outstanding of them, the abbé Jean Paul, new quarters were occupied in 1724, and in the following decade printing of the catalogues was begun. But this, however, was not completed. At the end of the period under consideration the library had a staff of no less than 54 people. Some measure of the high level of the demands made upon them can be gained from the lecture *The Duties and Qualifications of a Librarian*,[4] which the abbé Cotton des Houssayes delivered in 1780 at the Sorbonne.

The foregoing chapter has already said something about classification and cataloguing. The Enlightenment devoted itself with special energy to this task, above all in France. Bacon's division of all human knowledge[5] affected thinkers almost disastrously, for it implanted the dogma of the exhaustive classification of the fields of knowledge. One scheme followed another, a few acquiring some importance. But in practice these various successive proposals were avoided, and librarians stuck conservatively to the five divisions beloved in France (theology, jurisprudence, arts and sciences, belles lettres, and history). This division underlay Clément's classes; it was the one cultivated by Martin, the leading Parisian bookseller; and the Encyclopedists, by mentioning with praise the so-called "system of the booksellers of Paris," enhanced its reputation.

At first, public access to the library could be had only with difficulty; the abbé Bignon was the first to draw up rules making the use of the library considerably easier. In this way all the leaders of the Enlightenment were able to make use of the Royal Library, and furthermore the National Assembly of 1790 recognized its importance for French intellectual life. Its connections with historical studies never broke off. A special genealogical section was created for studying the family history of the nobility. Furthermore, the Cabinet des Chartes,[6] in whose establishment the Maurists played a prominent role, was united with the Royal Library, though at first quite informally.

Despite all this, it would be going too far to attribute to the institution as early as this a purely scientific character. As yet the conception of the library as a luxurious showplace had by no means been overthrown. When it came to buying or to soliciting gifts, precious items and rarities were much preferred. The library even had two separate divisions for prints and medals, upon which its royal owners lavished very special attention.

In England things were essentially no different. There, too, among those people who set the standards for libraries, most of the ideas which had been characteristic of the preceding period still prevailed. But progress did not occur the same way on opposite sides of the Channel. In France it was the person of the King about whom all efforts aiming at improvement centered; in England it was the whole nation, represented by Parliament. In France, as we have seen, the impulse sprang from the historians, in England from the natural philosophers. In the movement the Bodleian

Library did not play any prominent role. To be sure, it was not neglected after its splendid start: indeed it was enriched by many gifts. But during the Enlightenment the universities were not the center of English intellectual life; the capital city of London alone qualifies for consideration as such.

The plan to establish a large library in London had already made its appearance several times during the sixteenth century. About the middle of the next century, in the turbulent days of the Revolution, John Dury, keeper of the King's private collection, was occupied with library problems. This original thinker published in 1650 *The Reformed Librarie Keeper*, characterized him as "factor and trader for helps to learning," and went on to develop points of view which sound like anticipations of modern public library endeavors. The idea—not yet directly advocated by Dury—of developing the Royal Library into a public institution comes out later in Richard Bentley, who was directing this library about the turn of the century. He wrote out *A Proposal for building a Royal Library and establishing it by Act of Parliament*, and he also proposed a guarantee of a fixed yearly sum of money, one so large, in fact, that the collection could be increased to 200,000 volumes. But it was not until more than a generation later that a part of his ideas was put into operation; this was effected by the physicist Sir Hans Sloane, who was personal physician to the King.

Sloane succeeded the great Newton as President of the Royal Society. Dubbed by a satirist "the foremost toyman of his time," he collected everything which was "rare and curious," but which at the same time promoted "the enlargement of our knowledge in the works of nature," and so gathered rare animals, plants, and minerals, and also antiquities and considerable collections of books and manuscripts. In his will he created a group of trustees for his collections and consigned them to the nation in return for a sum to be paid to his heirs. In 1753 Parliament accepted the offer and united with the Sloane Collection two others—the Cottonian and Harleian Libraries. Sir Robert Bruce Cotton, a friend of Bodley's, had acquired extremely valuable materials on English history, which his grandson Robert presented to the nation in 1700, but which later suffered heavy damage by fire. Of the very valuable collection of Robert Harley (d. 1724), the books had already been sold, but now Parliament bought the manuscripts. Finally, to add to all this, George II donated his private library. The royal collection, from its inception in the Middle Ages, had had a checkered career—enrichments at the hands of the bibliophile Henry VII, losses during the period of the iconoclastic riots.[7] It owed much to Prince Henry, son of James I, and had benefited since 1662 from the copyright system, which now applied to the national library.

After the British Museum, thus created, had acquired a worthy home by the purchase of Montagu House, it was opened in 1759. The statutes provided "free access to all studious and curious persons"; in point of fact, access was made difficult by all sorts of formalities. In general, as its very name indicates, the British Museum was to be less a place for study than for exhibition, all the more because at the time its natural history collections still formed the more important part of its holdings. Hence it is understandable too that the first three Principal Librarians should be physicians and members of the royal Society.

During the foregoing epoch, Italy had continued to stand in the front rank along with France and England in library matters. Since the middle of the seventeenth century, however, it had rather slipped into the background. Nevertheless, even here there was no lack of scholarly movements from which libraries profited.

It was Muratori, working first in the Ambrosian Library, and after 1700 librarian and archivist for the Este in Modena who brought the Maurist methods of study to the Italian peninsula and thus founded the great historical and antiquarian school which occupied itself with the most diverse fields of research throughout the eighteenth century. Another member of the circle represented by Muratori and the Maurists was the Tuscan court librarian, Magliabech. An eccentric bachelor of repulsive appearance, he was the butt of Florentine jibes, yet as a scholar he enjoyed a worldwide reputation and carried on an international correspondence with the most outstanding men of the time. He was possessed by true bibliomania. In his home books were piled right up to the ceiling, and he could only find what he was looking for by virtue of a remarkable memory. Mabillon called him "a walking museum and a kind of living library" (*museum inambulans et viva quaedam bibliotheca*). At his death (1714) he left his collection to the Grand Duke and therewith laid the groundwork for the present-day Biblioteca Nazionale in Florence.[8]

Of other libraries which were founded, two deserve special mention: the library at Rome of Cardinal Casanate, a friend of Mabillon and Baluze, and the Brera Library at Milan, the founding of which took place in 1770 under the auspices of the Empress Maria Theresa quite in the spirit of the Enlightenment. Two exemplary accomplishments testify to the genuine scholarship then to be found in the ranks of Italian librarians—Bandini's manuscript catalogue for the Laurentian Library at Florence, and (even though it did remain unfinished), Audifreddi's catalogue of books for the aforementioned Biblioteca Casanatense.

Now if we turn our attention to Germany, we shall meet with much greater detail than in the lands just reviewed. This is conditioned, for one thing, by the plan of our book, which prescribes a closer examination of German than of other libraries. There is, however, a second reason to be adduced, which comes into play just at this point in our exposition. After 1650 Germany took a most active part in the intellectual movements of the West, even though the frightful wounds which the Thirty Years' War had inflicted upon her healed right slowly. As a consequence, up to the end of our period there prevailed in many libraries conditions little worthy of a nation great in culture, whereas during the same time other libraries whipped themselves into shape so effectively as to surpass by far in importance even what had been achieved in Paris.

There exist two accounts of German libraries: one that of Uffenbach at the beginning, the other that of Hirsching at the end of the eighteenth century. Both paint a pretty cheerless picture of the majority of institutions open to the public: insufficient space, defective classification, incomplete catalogues, bad conditions of use. These descriptions are not complete, nor do they appear free from prejudice; nevertheless, for the most part, they would seem to portray actual conditions.

Church libraries of any importance were still to be found only in the larger cities. The libraries of religious foundations and monasteries were often wholly neglected. The tendencies of the Enlightenment led to the selling of old parchment codices—for example, the treasures of the monastery of Weissenburg were in danger of being sold to goldsmiths. Only the intervention of people with insight saved them and made possible their preservation at Wolfenbüttel. But conditions were not like this everywhere. A whole series of Frankish and Bavarian monasteries, we know, took stock of their collections once more and reclassified them and even found money for acquiring new books. Also, new buildings were not lacking—I mention only the charming rococo building at Amorbach. And in the Black Forest monastery of St. Blasien there developed under the influence of the Maurists scholarly activity which under the learned Abbott Gerbert reached its climax shortly before the Revolution.

Most of the municipal libraries dragged out miserable existences; a few basked in the glory of previously acquired riches. One can credit new life only to a few cities which were then on the upgrade. At Frankfurt am Main the collections which had hitherto existed separately were merged in 1668 to form a public library, and the post of librarian was created somewhat later. Leipzig in 1677 received by private bequest a municipal library, which was later enlarged and developed. The most unusual creation was the Hamburg commercial Library (Hamburger Kommerz-bibliothek) in the year 1735. This owed its origin to the members of the merchant class, and accordingly concentrated upon important literature having to do with trade and shipping, and along with these collected local material on Hamburg.

One of the heartening phenomena in library affairs at this time was the resurgence of the private library. In this sphere the evil effects of the wars could be most swiftly remedied. Indeed, setting up such libraries expressed the general spirit of the times. In Uffenbach's account their significance already comes clearly to the fore, and

Figure 34: 18th century drawing of the National Library in Vienna.

Hirsching notes that they have considerably increased in number and quality. Berlin and Nuremberg had the largest number of private libraries, with Hamburg, Dresden, and Vienna not far behind. The cabinet of curiosities was not yet totally abandoned, but the scholarly character of the collections grew steadily stronger. Scientific or semi-scientific books formed the largest part of the collections, while belles-lettres were but little cultivated. As for the court libraries of the princes, they too, for the most part, preserved that typical mixture of exhibition room and study room which had come into being during the previous period.

The Court Library at Vienna developed into one of the most splendid collections of rarities in Europe. Its ascendancy began with the summoning of Lambeck, who was a native of Hamburg. He had traveled widely, made international connections in the learned world, and acquired for himself a reputation as a universal scholar. From 1663 to 1680 he labored at Vienna, and there he carried through a reclassification of the collections. Cataloguing, however, never got beyond the project stage; the descriptions of manuscripts which he gave in his *Commentrarii* were too minute and in no way even comparable to Montfaucon's *catalogue raisonné*. In general Lambeck was addicted to promising more than he was in a position to carry out. The influx of books and manuscripts which had set in about the middle of the seventeenth century became even greater in the following century under the rule of the Emperor Charles VI. At that time the magnificent collections of Prince Eugene of Savoy were added, and the library acquired new and excellent quarters, the work of Master Fischer von Erlach.

The library at Berlin founded by the Great Elector had its ups and downs. Under his immediate successors the collection was further enlarged and the basis of its later wealth in Orientalia established. Also, in 1699, following the example of France, the legal deposit system was put into force. Evil days arrived with the rule of the Soldier King, Frederick William of Prussia, who stopped the salaries of the staff and turned over part of the library funds to one of his generals. In fact, the book-stock was in danger of being given away to other institutions. Even Frederick the Great, for whom daily communion with books was vitally important, who set up separate libraries in his various castles, and was always accompanied by a traveling library, showed very little interest in the Royal Library for a long time. It was not until after 1770 that his attitude changed. Then large funds for buying books were provided, so that the number of volumes climbed in a short time to 150,000, and to house them a new building, the famous Kommode, was erected. But even so, the internal organization did not improve, for the staff required to administer the collection properly was lacking.

One of the admirers of Frederick the Great was Charles Eugene of Württemberg. He was a true representative of reckless, enlightened absolutism. In addition to the

Karlsschule[9] he also founded a public library which, thanks to his industry as a collector, contained about 100,000 volumes when he died in 1793. The Duke made his own decisions and personally dispatched all the business of the library, working at this less in the interest of his realm than of his own personal reputation. Naturally he placed the greatest value upon rarities, and especially upon his collection of Bibles. The following incident illustrates how highly the princes of those days valued their rare books: when Professor Michaelis of Göttingen asked for the use of a Hebrew Bible codex from Cassel in 1767, the Landgrave granted him permission, but had the manuscript brought to Göttingen under the protection of a squadron of hussars.

At this point a word about the library at St. Petersburg is in order. In his efforts to assimilate Russian culture to that of the West, Peter the Great was already thinking of founding such an institution. But it was Catherine II, the admirer of Voltaire, who actually put the plan into operation. The nucleus consisted of the Warsaw collection of the brothers Zaluski. These Polish nobles had served their people well in the revival of literature and science, and had also collected a library of more than 100,000 volumes, which they turned over to public use in 1748. Thereafter, however, it fell into decline and neglect until it was carried off to St. Petersburg as a prize of war. Among the St. Petersburg library's later additions was the collection of Dubrovsky, an official of the Russian embassy in Paris, who had acquired all sorts of treasures from French monasteries during the Revolution, outstanding among them manuscripts from Corbie. During the nineteenth century the St. Petersburg library was frequently enlarged in the same way. Always the results were splendid. Today it is one of the richest and most outstanding libraries in the world.[10]

Of the reproaches which Uffenbach hurled against German libraries, the bitterest indeed concerned the incompetence of their personnel. He denounced them as ignorant, discourteous, envious, and lazy. Hirsching's characterization is equally unflattering: they have little or no knowledge of books; they are arrogant misanthropes who look upon their positions as sinecures. As a matter of fact, in this respect both commentators seemed to have been not entirely unjustified. Even Lessing, when he was called to Wolfenbüttel in 1770, had it in mind to use the library rather than allow himself to be used by it. Consequently he neglected his job and, though he did initiate a reclassification, it ended in general disorder.

Nevertheless it must be stressed that not all librarians shared Lessing's point of view. The sharp criticisms which as we have seen, often became loud, the reproachful epithets such as "Cerberus" or "Dragon of the Golden Fleece" which occur fairly often in contemporary literature, show that there was another school of thought. Indeed, on the very spot where Lessing spent his last years there had been work two generations before the man who is looked upon as the leader of the German Enlightenment, a man who laid down excellent principles governing the duties of a librarian. This man was Gottfried Wilhelm Leibniz.

As a boy Leibniz had already taken a lively interest in his father's book-collection. When in later years he became the librarian of the learned bibliophile Von Boineburg of Mainz, he broached for the first time his favorite bibliographical project—to issue, after the fashion of the *Journal des Savants*, a "semi-annual selection of books" (*nucleus librarius semestralis*) and to cumulate these lists into "an inventory of the human knowledge contained in books" (*inventarium scientiae humanae libris proditae*). It was his belief that true advance of knowledge was possible only when each individual scholar could quickly and conveniently run over the sum total of previous accomplishments.

A decisive influence upon Leibniz was his stay in Paris, since this came precisely at the time of the brilliant advance of the Royal Library under Colbert. Clément and Baluze were numbered among his friends, and, along with other things, he read Naudé's *Avis*. From this time, too, dated Leibniz's close relations with the learned Jesuits and the Maurists. His historical studies, which inaugurated a new era in German historical research, moved entirely in the tracks which they had laid down. A real and important consequence of these researches was his steadily deepening understanding of the importance of the scholarly library.

In 1676 Leibniz was called to Hanover as librarian and historiographer, and fifteen years later he also assumed direction of the Wolfenbüttel library. Both institutions owed to him a large increase in their collections, and Wolfenbüttel in particular the creation of an alphabetical catalogue and the erection of a new building, an oval central structure with a skylight dome that aroused much admiration. But Leibniz deserves such a pre-eminent place in the history of libraries not so much for his practical accomplishments as for the principles, ideas, and projects contained in his correspondence and in his numerous proposals to the Guelphic princes.

The ideal Leibniz envisaged was a complete, well-administered book-collection, and with a continual variety of figures of speech and changing imagery he strove to delineate its importance. He compared it with a gathering of the greatest men of all ages and races who communicate to us their most select thoughts. Such a library should fulfill for state and society functions similar to church and school. He measured the value of a library, not by the number, but by the quality of its books, and desired in this respect not rarities but rather "key" works of those authors who had performed worthy services for the republic of letters. Small, "curieuse" volumes he thought more important than thick tomes with contents devoid of sense. The heaviest emphasis he laid upon regular acquisition of continuations and new books: neglect of this

IV. 16.   *Nach Schoits. gez. u. lith. v. E. Zimmermann.*   B. II.

G. W. Freiherr v. Leibnitz.

Figure 35: Gottfried Wilhelm Leibniz (1646–1716), historian, philosopher, and librarian, played an important role in the development of libraries as we know them today.

practice would involve the decline of the entire collection. A necessary presupposition for all this, however, was the availability of an adequate yearly appropriation. For this Leibniz never left off besieging the Guelphic princes with appeals, and kept hatching new methods for creating the necessary sources of income. In problems of classification and cataloguing, too, he showed his practical insight. Like the French librarians he preferred a strictly scholarly system, the "civil classification according to the faculties and the professions" (*division civile selon les facultés et les professions*). He favored the alphabetical catalogue, but desired also a chronological arrangement by year of publication, and recommended especially subject indexes (*indices materiarum*) arranged by catchword.

Many of Leibniz's ideas occur already in Naudé's *Avis*, others in Dury and Bently. But this leaves undiminished the merit of his contribution, which consists of having clearly presented the importance of the large scholarly reference library and pointed out ways and means to its development.[11] It would be a pleasant task to trace in detail the effect which Leibniz had upon his contemporaries and later generations. Here, naturally, we can trace this influence only to a few places.

It is likely that with Leibniz's cooperation recommendations concerning cataloguing and acquisition were sent from Hanover to Helmstedt, but because of the inefficiency of the librarian there, they were never put into effect. In 1724, a pupil and former assistant of Leibniz, Eckhart, came to Würzburg. The Frankish university library owed to his initiative a systematic classification and cataloguing of the collection, the creation of a regular budget, as well as liberal rules for the use of the library.

Not so easy to discern is the way in which Leibniz's ideas permeated to the capital of Saxony. Dresden's wealth of private libraries has already been mentioned. At this time collecting books was fashionable, particularly among the upper classes. By far the best example was set by Count Brühl, who brought together a most valuable collection of 62,000 volumes. Among his rivals in politics as well as bibliophily was Count Bünau. In contrast to Count Brühl, his love of books arose out of no desire for ostentation, but primarily out of scholarly motives. He spent this leisure hours pursuing historical researches in the manner of Leibniz and the Maurists, and no less a figure than Winckelmann was his secretary. Bünau's great history of the German Empire and its emperors had an enthusiastic reception and earned him the reputation of a German Muratori. His book-collection arose in connection with these historical studies. It had a universal character, even though it was second to Brühl's in size.

From 1740 on Francke was in the service of the Count and, at the instigation and under the direction of his master, he published the *Catalogus Bibliothecae Bunavianae*. Although this work was not completed, it acquired a reputation far beyond German territories, above all for its original subdivisions, which were determined chiefly by historical and geographical principles. When in the sixties, the collections of Bünau and Brühl were merged with the Dresden Court Library, Francke entered its service and carried through a grand reclassification according to the principles tested under Bünau. His work was continued by the historian Adelung. At this time the library received a new home in the Japanese Palace, catalogues hitherto lacking were created, and money necessary for acquiring books was readily provided.

Although Dresden at the end of this century ranked among the most important German libraries, the Göttingen University Library enjoyed a much higher reputation—and justly so, for it represented not only the most complete realization of Leibniz's program but an advance upon it by virtue of its close connection with the university, built up quite in accordance with modern principles. It was Baron Von Münchhausen, Göttingen's first curator, who "saw from the beginning what influence the library must have upon the whole nature of a university" and who "immediately laid plans to provide the university with a character of its own by means of the library."

A glance at the other university libraries of Germany reveals the unique position of Göttingen at this time. According to Hirsching, the situation was satisfactory or tolerable in only a few universities; in the majority, conditions were either permanently or temporarily downright wretched. In one the collection was not accessible because the librarian was out of town, or the librarian's sickness kept the library closed all winter. In another the rooms were dark, with broken windows covered by spider-webs, and filled with soot or mold. In a third the books were so shelved that getting at them required the agility of a tightrope walker or a roofer. In Halle itself, where German rationalism originated, deplorable conditions existed even after the middle of the eighteenth century, primarily because there philological and historical studies were not adequately pursued, whereas they were among the most important disciplines at Göttingen.

Until his death in 1770, Von Münchhausen took personal charge of buying books, arranged to be represented at all important auctions, and kept up a steady business with foreign and domestic book-dealers. Consideration was always given to wishes of the professors. In addition, Von Münchhausen was able to induce large gifts. These activities proceeded according to the principles laid down by Leibniz, and every branch of knowledge received its due. The new books which arrived during the course of the year were placed at the disposal of the reviewers of the *Göttinger Gelehrte Anzeigen*, for one of the aims of Von Münchhausen was close cooperation between the library and this university publication, which speedily became known and esteemed throughout the entire learned world.

The actual director of the library was Professor Gesner. Of him his biographer says: "He was by far the first among librarians, not only in knowledge, but in most elegant civility and in the courtesy which he showed toward visitors."[12] In one of his own reports Gesner laid down the requirement that the librarian must not, like a financier, merely accumulate capital consisting of books, but must share his wealth with as many as possible. Gesner was regarded as one of the founders of Neo-Humanist philology; after him its leader was Heyne. Before his call to Göttingen in 1763 Heyne had held a position in the library of Count Brühl, and had been on familiar terms with Winckelmann. At Göttingen he developed into an organizer on a grand scale who with sure penetration found the most practical solution for every problem. He combined in his own person the productivity of both Von Münchhausen and Gesner and thereby strengthened even more the influence of these two. The book-collection, which amounted to about 60,000 volumes when he took office, doubled within the next twenty years and around the turn of the century reached the 200,000 mark. At the outset the library had occupied a room of the lecture building; in the course of time it took over the whole building and made necessary the added construction of a wing.

In cataloguing a strictly scientific classification was rejected as a matter of course and, as Leibniz had recommended, a practical scheme used. Yet the creation of the cataloguing system did not fare well at the start: many costly mistakes were made. It was not until after 1782, when Heyne had found an excellent collaborator in the person of Reuss, that they succeeded in creating a close organic connection between the arrangement of books on the shelf and the catalogue, and in making sure that every new book went through a regular process in which it was entered in the accession book and in the author and subject catalogues.

At the end of the eighteenth century the fame of the Göttingen book-collection was on every tongue. It would be easy to bring together a whole choir of eulogists, among them the most illustrious minds such as Herder, Goethe, and Von Humboldt. However, others maintained that the proud Göttingen professors owed their scholarly successes solely to the university library.

Chapter VIII.

The French Revolution And The Nineteenth Century

Since the end of the Middle Ages the development of libraries had moved with a clearly recognizable rhythm. After the Renaissance, libraries found themselves faced with the task of solving hitherto unknown problems of internal organization; and again after the Enlightenment had produced the type of the scholarly reference library, the nineteenth century found itself harried by a series of grave new problems of organization. As the Renaissance was ushered in, large numbers of books had been transferred to new owners, and this took place at the beginning of the Enlightenment to an even greater degree. In the earlier age the Reformation had provided the impetus; now it was the French Revolution.

In November, 1789 the libraries of the Church in France were declared national property. Three years later the collections of émigrés were confiscated. It is estimated that eight million books in France parted from their owners at this time, almost two million in Paris alone. Then it became a problem to make these piles of books safe, to classify them, and to bring them into general use. The successive revolutionary governments passed a long series of laws and administrative decrees, and even planned a great French union catalogue. But times were too unsettled for action to follow upon resolve. There was much waste and destruction. In general, large quantities of books landed first in temporary storehouses, the *dépôts littéraires*, and from there in the new district libraries, the administration of which was entrusted to municipal officials in 1803, while the government retained supervisory powers. But for a long time the state of these communal libraries (*bibliothèques communales*) still left much to be desired.

Not until toward the middle of the century was a general system put into effect through decrees from Paris, followed somewhat later by reorganization of the university libraries.[1]

Nine *dépôts littéraires* had been established in the capital. Out of them came additional book-collections for the new state institutions, the Arsenal, the Sainte Geneviève, the Mazarine Library, and, most important of all, the Bibliothèque Nationale. The holdings of the Bibliothèque Nationale increased by about 300,000 books, as well as many thousands of manuscripts, among them the treasures of St. Germain-des-Prés and the Sorbonne. The provinces also had to pay their tribute to the Bibliothèque Nationale, and when troops of the Republic and the Empire carried victorious arms to the Netherlands, Germany, Austria, and Italy, many valuable items traveled to Paris from the libraries of these countries, only part of them to return home after Napoleon's fall. A decree of 1805 had ordered that the Bibliothèque Nationale should be made as complete as possible from the resources of the remaining libraries of the land, in exchange for its own duplicates. Although this order was never fully carried out, since that time the principle has been upheld that the Bibliothèque Nationale must be the chief library of France not merely in name but in fact. With the same object, the ancient laws relating to legal deposit of copies were renewed and strengthened.[2]

This short sketch of the fortunes of the Bibliothèque Nationale would be incomplete without mention of the great services of Joseph Van Praen, who was at this time director of the Department of Printed Books. Credit is due to him first and foremost for taking advantage of all opportunities created by the events of the time. It was his leadership in the main that helped to put into effect the government's resolve to make this new state institution available to everyone. He alone—thanks to a remarkable memory—could find his way among the stored-up treasures, and he richly deserved to be called "the living catalogue" (*le catalogue vivant*).

The Revolution had two very important results for French library history—centralization of book-collections and the principle that books were to be accessible to the general public. Let us now see how Germany followed the example of her neighbor.

The dissolution of the Jesuit Order in Germany had already caused a noticeable transfer of large numbers of books. Now many of the other churches and monasteries began to dispose of their treasures, so that eager bibliophiles and dealers in books and manuscripts who knew their business had a profitable time. Typical of the times was the former Benedictine Maugérard, who outwitted all his colleagues by artful dodges, and moreover had no scruples about unsavory dealings.

From 1794 on there were visitations of libraries along the Rhine by French agents. At the start of the new century Maugérard was one of these agents, and he gleaned so thoroughly and used his knowledge and experience so unflaggingly in the service of his Parisian employers that a tablet was later erected to perpetuate his name. Only items of minor value found their way to the *dépôts littéraires* which had now too been set up on German soil. The regions of Germany which the defeat of Prussia first exposed to the foe suffered no such losses. Only a few collections, like that at Wolfenbüttel, saw part of their holdings temporarily removed to Paris. Göttingen, the most important library of the new kingdom of Westphalia, remained completely intact. In fact, Jerome Bonaparte planned to do with Göttingen in a small way what his brother had striven to carry out at the Bibliothèque Nationale on a large scale. But the books sent to Göttingen from abroad were hardly unpacked when the collapse of the French regime forced their return.

For the remaining libraries of Germany the Principal Decree of the Imperial Deputation in 1803 was decisive.[3] With the disappearance of a host of principalities and city republics, a good many of their libraries vanished from the scene or changed masters. Most important of all, just as in France, seizure of church libraries was now effected.

Secularization achieved its best results in Bavaria, and Munich benefitted especially. A short time before, when the crown had passed to the Palatine line, the very large holdings of the Mannheim library had been transferred to Munich. Now, under the prudent and (despite certain errors) unexceptionable direction of Von Aretin, about 150 church and monastic collections found their way to the capital. As a result the Hofbibliothek at Munich held the leadership among court libraries for a long time, and its wealth in medieval manuscripts and incunabula may well remain forever unsurpassed. In addition to Munich, the Bavarian government provided especially handsomely for Bamberg and Würzburg. Things went correspondingly well, though on a more modest scale, in Württemburg and Baden, where the collections of Stuttgart and Karlsruhe enjoyed considerable growth. The same was true, finally, of Hessen-Darmstadt, while in Nassau, for the most part, resources were squandered in criminal fashion.

For Prussia secularization was no such epoch-making event because the Catholic domain formed but the smaller part of her territory. Moreover, there was no plan of any kind for centralization which would benefit Berlin: only a few of the duplicates which were sent out by the provinces reached that city. More worthy of notice is the growth of resources at Münster and Königsberg and, above all, Breslau. The university was moved from Frankfurt an der Oder to Breslau, and along with it came its book-collection. Thereupon it was planned to make Breslau into a central library like those at Munich and Paris. The transfer of church collections to this library, it is true, was soon stopped, yet the Breslau library received about 70,000 volumes, among them a large number of incunabula.

The changes which have been described produced the problem of making usable these institutions, some of them newly born, some importantly enriched. This task shaped up all the harder because at the same time demands upon libraries had grown heavier—for the following reasons. In the first place, in Germany deepening national consciousness and change in social organization caused libraries generally to be looked upon as public institutions. Then again, the new century brought an increase in scholarly activities by which libraries could not remain unaffected. But they showed themselves quite unprepared for it, as can be understood from the points made in the last chapter. There was practically no such thing as a class of trained librarians. Still, there were two libraries whose organization served as useful models—Dresden and Göttingen.

The Göttingen system now swept triumphantly through Germany. It was carried over into the Prussian university libraries, and so into the newly founded libraries of Bonn and Breslau. That it was put into operation in Berlin, too was due to Wilhelm von Humboldt, who as a student at Göttingen had eagerly cultivated the friendship of Heyne, and who now, in the rebirth of Prussia, assumed decisive leadership of the educational system, even if only for a year. The University of Berlin was founded at this time, and as a consequence the responsibilities of the Royal Library expanded greatly.[4] Through Humboldt's initiative the yearly budget increased, the organizational structure improved, and more liberal arrangements for using the library went into effect. The new alphabetical catalogue stuck close to the Göttingen model. On the other hand, a couple of decades later Schrader used his own methods in setting up a classed catalogue. Since that time the Prussian State Library has had an administrative tool which neither the British Museum nor the Bibliothèque Nationale yet possesses.[5]

At Berlin conditions were relatively simple. But how was the sister institution at Munich to overcome its much stiffer problems?

At first there was an attempt to group by subject the manuscripts which had been acquired, but this track was fortunately abandoned in time. It was Schmeller's great contribution not only to have insured continuation of the historical tradition by reestablishing the principle of providence but also to have carried out the cataloguing and shelving according to this principle during the years from 1829 to 1852. Treading in his footsteps, his students and followers could then publish the monumental Munich catalogue of manuscripts.[6]

The same thing happened with the newly acquired books. Here too a few unlucky experiments were made at first until there appeared in Schrettinger just the person to come to the rescue. A keen practical mind, Schrettinger derived from an unsuccessful trial of the Göttingen system the realization that imitation would not lead him to his goal and that the special problem which he faced required a solution of its own. Consequently he classified his mass of books in coordinated groups which he then combined into a few main classes, and completed the alphabetical catalogue up to the year 1818. His other plans were far ahead of his time; some were blocked by the opposition of colleagues and others were never carried out completely. But Schrettinger left them to posterity in this theoretical writings. In them we find also the fundamental theme: "to dispel the chimaera of detailed technique is to lay the foundation of a genuine library science."

Among the opponents of this point of view was F.A. Ebert. He had been trained at Dresden, had steeped himself thoroughly in the system of Francke, and had made it his ideal. Consequently, appointed to head the Wolfenbüttel collection in 1823, he began to reclassify without proper regard to local conditions; then, before the work was done, he returned to Dresden and there—though barely forty—met his death by falling from a ladder. If, in the light of the above, Ebert's practical accomplishments were of little value, his literary achievements deserve all the greater consideration. We can only mention here his history of the Dresden library, based scrupulously upon reliable sources, his bibliographical dictionary, worked out with careful scholarship,[7] and his original treatise on manuscripts, which grew out of his work with the Wolfenbüttel treasures. We must glance for a moment at his youthful essay *On Public Libraries*.[8] Here he waxes sarcastic over university library conditions which were still the rule at the beginning of the nineteenth century, describing the libraries as "dusty, desolate, and unfrequented rooms in which the librarian must spend a few hours weekly to discharge his duties—so that during this time he can be alone!" From this he passes on to proposals for reform, of which the most important asserts: "The hitherto existing practice of librarianship as a part-time affair must be done away with. The proper direction of a public library requires persons endowed with the finest qualities of mind and character, who will bring their abilities to bear on the task before them." These ideas are found again in a more profound and expanded form in a later work, *The Training of the Librarian.*[9]

"I spend my own energies serving others" (*aliis inserviendo consumor*) was to be the motto of every capable library worker, according to Ebert, and Schrettinger furnished a public example of this point of view. Where these two differed was in their working methods. Schrettinger, pre-eminently a practical man, had derived new principles from a great new problem; Ebert, the theorizer, remaining for the most part steeped in the ideas of the past century, held fast to the ideals of Francke.

Both Schrettinger and Ebert, however, struggled virtually alone in their day. It would be incorrect to deny altogether in this epoch of poets and thinkers any true interest in the internal organization of libraries: the efforts of Goethe in behalf of the institutions at Jena and Weimar which had been placed under his supervision argue just to the contrary.[10] But it appears in general as if the orientation of knowledge at the time actually made difficult a true understanding of the situation on the part of the educated classes from which the library officials were usually recruited. Even if we consider as an exception the notion of Hoffmann von Fallersleben, curator of the University of Breslau Library, who saw in his office only a sinecure and declared the rigorous demands for service made upon him oppressive and worse than the worst corporal punishment of eighteenth century army discipline, it still remains significant on the whole that the new professional periodical, the *Serapeum*, ventured to publish his opinions in 1840.

The all-powerful library committee was a disastrous creation, for it led mostly to the already meager funds being earmarked for the use of special faculties, or indeed of individual professors.[11] At Tübingen the Professor of Constitutional Law, Robert von Mohl, came up against especially bad conditions of this kind. He waged a sturdy fight against them, and in 1836 took over the direction of the library himself. His words show the conception of the duties of the new office which animated him: "the chief librarian, whatever else he may be, must think and plan night and day for his library; in its behalf he must buy and exchange, beg and—one might almost add—steal." But he met strong opposition from his colleagues and the administration, and failed in his attempt to eliminate the influence of the library committee and to regulate the expenditure of funds by uniform and reasonable principles.

The next decades brought the Revolution and then the Reaction. The times were not suitable for fundamental library reforms, which came only after conditions in general had changed. In order to evaluate them properly, however, it is necessary to have some acquaintance with contemporary events in England and France, more particularly with the development of the British Museum and the Bibliothèque Nationale.

The great reform of the British Museum is bound up with the personality of the Italian, Sir Anthony Panizzi. He was not a scholar, though we do have valuable works from his hand, such as the editions of Bojardo, but he devoted himself wholly to public life and took a most active part in politics. Passionate by nature—he had been forced to flee his native land as a Carbonaro—and faced with opposition from many sides in his new position in a foreign land, he lived a fight, yet carried it on not from any personal motives but only in the interests of the institution to which he had dedicated his powers and which he believed himself alone capable of leading to the desired eminence. His contemporaries called him the second founder of the British Museum, the Napoleon of librarians. Garnett, his successor, said of him: "Panizzi governed the library as his friend Cavour governed his country, and in a spirit and with objectives nearly similar, perfecting its internal organization with the one hand while he extended its frontiers with the other."

Panizzi's steady rise—in 1831 he became Extra-Assistant, in 1837 Keeper of Printed Books, finally in 1856 Principal Librarian—only signifies a steady extension of the range of his influence. In reports to the trustees, in oral and written transactions with government commissions, even in social contacts with friends and acquaintances, he fought for his principles, which he had early in his career summarized in the following three sentences: "The (British) Museum is not a show, but an institution for the diffusion of culture. It is a department of the civil service, and should be conducted in the spirit of other public departments. It should be managed with the utmost possible liberality." What this meant for his time is shown by the remark of the contemporary member of Parliament, Cobbett: The British Museum is a place where the rich and the aristocrats go to amuse themselves by reading. Let them pay for their own amusement.[12]

Since its origin, the British Museum's holdings in books and manuscripts had been expanded on a large scale, thanks especially to large and frequent gifts, such as the King's Library, the favorite project of George III. Also, from time to time, Parliament had approved additional appropriations. System and continuity, however, were lacking. Panizzi took the position that the British Museum was called upon to become a national library worthy of a nation like England. It should preserve all English books and the most important foreign literature. Consequently he made sure of a large and regular yearly budget, the appropriation of which was not continent upon conditions of any kind. The result was that the book-collection quickly doubled, and about 1870 it had already reached 1,000,000 volumes. At the same time he was instrumental in obtaining valuable gifts, notably that of his friend, Grenville. Finally, entirely through his personal insistence and despite all opposition, he brought about strict enforcement of the copyright provisions, which had hitherto been administered very negligently.[13]

Panizzi applied himself with similar industry to the problem of cataloguing, which was pressing for solution just at the time he entered the Museum. He opposed the classed catalogue which had already been begun and succeeded in getting an alphabetical catalogue started. For this he drew up rules which before long came to be regarded as canons in the Anglo-Saxon library world. Publication of the catalogue had to be discontinued at first after a premature attempt had been made in deference to the wishes of the trustees, and work under Panizzi's direction was completed only in manuscript; nevertheless printing of the catalogue in later years (1881-1900) was carried through entirely in the spirit of its creator.

Panizzi has a special claim to high repute because of the building changes and additions made to the British Museum in his day. At a time when the continent stuck to the old hall-with-gallery type of building and exerted itself only to increase its dimensions, as the fantastic creations of the Frenchman Horeau illustrate, when even America could not bring herself to abandon this tradition, Panizzi took the step required by circumstances and separated the rooms used for shelving books and the rooms used by readers. Strongly impressed, in all probability, by the recently completed Crystal Palace, which had shown the dazzling possibilities of iron construction, in 1852 he himself drew up the plan for the reading room. When the building was finished five years later, the height of its dome and its spaciousness aroused universal admiration: it fell short of the Roman Pantheon by only a very little, and it provided accommodation for several hundred readers.

The new stack space surrounded the reading room. The principle on which the stacks were constructed had already been enunciated by a writer in Frankfurt, but had attracted no real attention at the time. Gärtner's beautiful building for the Munich library had gone only as far as constructing the galleries low enough to enable the impractical ladders to be dispensed with. In the British Museum the sections of stack had removable shelves, and fire-proofing was achieved by the use of iron exclusively. The greatest efforts, however, were expended upon saving space by setting the of library buildings.

The first imitation of this British Museum model came in Paris with the extensive enlargement of the Bibliothèque Nationale. This had become a crying need, since the enormous number of books which the Revolution had brought into the library and which had then grown slowly but steadily could now for the first time be arranged so as to form a view of the whole collection. First, after Van Praet's death in 1837, the old and already catalogued parts of the collection were grouped into a *fonds porté*; the uncatalogued books which had accrued sine 1789 and the later acquisitions were gathered into a *fonds non porté*; both *fonds* were then divided into the classes of the shelving scheme, which had descended essentially intact from Clément. Then the labor of cataloguing went forward and at first, just as across the Channel, there was an attempt at a classed catalogue. Some sections were completed and even got into print. But here too the path which had been entered upon did not lead to the desired goal. And what Panizzi had been for London and Schrettinger for Munich, Delisle became for Paris at this fateful moment.

Léopold Delisle was one of the most brilliant representatives of nineteenth-century French scholarship and, without ever occupying a professor's chair, he became the leader of a historical school. As a pupil at the École des Chartes he carried on, as it were, the traditions of the Maurists. Quite naturally, therefore, he devoted himself at first to the Department of Manuscripts, the cataloguing and classification of which is essentially his work. Probably to him even more than to Schmeller belongs the honor of being called the creator of the modern manuscript catalogue. Placed at the head of the library in 1847, Delisle demonstrated his ability as an organizer on a grand scale. He had already shown his determination a short time before by defending the collections against the attacks of the Commune. How well he combined scholarly acuteness with diplomatic skill is shown in the notorious case of Libri. That Italian scholar and adventurer, after having attained a high position in France, had used it to carry to astonishing lengths a plundering of the libraries of Paris and the provinces. The action brought against him became entangled with the political controversies of the year of the Revolution, 1848, and consequently resulted unsatisfactorily. It was not until some decades later that Delisle was able to produce indisputable proofs of the larceny and even to retrieve for France an important part of the stolen treasures.

As head of the library Delisle was to do for the Department of Printed Books what had already been done for the manuscripts. First, within each class he placed the new acquisitions in a special group, the *fonds nouveau,* within which the books were shelved simply by a running number (*numerus currens*). At the same time a list of new books—at first written, a bit later printed—began to be issued to the public. Then the still untouched parts *of the fonds non porté* were worked on, so that by 1893 everything in the library was recorded on cards. Three years later printing of the alphabetical catalogue began. Since then, despite many obstacles, it has been pressing forward steadily, even though the time of its completion is not yet in prospect.[14]

Now if we turn our attention back to Germany, the question forces itself upon us: was what occurred in Germany at the end of the nineteenth century influenced from abroad by the examples of Paris or London? As for Paris, the answer must be negative. Delisle, to be sure, had very active contacts with his colleagues across the Vosges, but Germany already had the completely adequate example of Munich, and (most important of all) the reorganization of the Bibliothèque Nationale came too late to be seriously considered as a model. It was different with regard to Panizzi. That striking personality embodied the ideal which Ebert and Von Mohl had once championed. We know today that those in authority in Germany were in touch with him; systematic research, in my opinion, will make clear the details of these relations. As a result, the new type of building created by Panizzi formed an essential part of the German program of reform, as we shall see.

At the head of this movement stood the philologist, Friedrich Ritschl of Bonn. His biographer has nothing but praise for his term as library director, comprising the years 1854-1865. The recent historian of the library of the University of Bonn, on the other hand, takes obvious pains to depreciate his merits. There is little doubt that he had many truly unpleasant characteristics. Nor do we owe to him any really trail-blazing innovations. But, fired by the example of the Alexandrian Library, which his own investigations had for the first time placed in its true light, he transformed the hitherto badly and rigidly administered Bonn library into a "well managed instrument of ready liberality."

Even more important, however, was the influence of Ritschl's personality. From the ranks of his subordinates and a host of volunteer assistants developed that school of librarians whose effectiveness revealed itself in the seventies. One of them was Klette, whose pamphlet *The Autonomy of the Profession of Librarianship*[15] contributed in no small measure to a break with the previous system. Another was Dziatzko, who, as Prussia's first professional librarian, reorganized the ill-managed Breslau library wholly in the spirit of his teacher, drew up the exemplary *Instructions* for the alphabetical card catalogue, and transferred to Göttingen in 1886, occupied there the newly created chair of Library Science.

Barack, founder and for many years director of the great new Strassburg collection, was a professional librarian. So, too, was Hartwig at Halle. Like Ritschl and Dziatzko he directed his attention chiefly to complete and up-to-date cataloguing of the collection. The fruits of his labors, the scheme of the Halle classed catalogue, won universal approval. His regime is important in another respect. In the years 1878-1880 came the new library building, which made use of the Anglo-French stack system for the first time in Germany. A whole series of additional new buildings followed, bringing into being the new and ever more practical type of lay-out: stack, administrative rooms, reading room, and periodical room. Attempts were made to combine esthetic with practical aims until finally in the Deutsche Bücherei at Leipzig, completed in 1916, the most fortunate answer to the problem was found.

But let us not hasten too far ahead of our period! The reform movement laid hold of ever-widening circles and even found strong support within the scholarly world. Realism had replaced idealism. Now the effort was to make sure of single facts by exact methods. In order to master such masses of subject-matter, large-scale organizations were created and progressive differentiation of research carried through. Each individual discipline provided itself with one or more special journals. In all this the library attained a much higher importance than ever before. To administer the collection efficiently and make it ready for use was, so to speak, a necessary element of the whole business of scholarship.

To this we must add that after the formation of the German Empire, with the consequent political and economic prosperity, considerably larger funds had been made available. Moreover, the development of trade and technology increased the possibilities of taking care of the expansion of book-collections just as far as the need of them grew. Finally, the government now also awoke to its obligations toward libraries.

No one was more aware of the importance of the library as a public institution than Althoff, who had been the moving spirit of the Prussian Ministry of Education since the eighties. In his still unwritten biography his efforts in behalf of libraries will take up a good deal of space.[16] We may even speak of an Althoff era. He fought most earnestly for the adequate financing of the institutions under his control. His next concern was for the library staff, its enlargement, improvement of its economic and social status, and finally for adequate training and regular employment. These efforts of the Ministry found support in the new professional journal founded by Hartwig (*Zentralblatt für Bibliothekswesen*) and in the library association (Verein Deutscher Bibliothekare) founded in 1900, with its annual meetings.

Naturally Althoff's actions especially benefited the Royal Library at Berlin. The year 1885 brought a reorganization in which its functions as a national institution were greatly expanded. Even if the desired end was not nearly attained, as we shall later see, yet the Royal Library now took a deserved first place among its German sister institutions. And that an occasional violation of the principle ordinarily followed of appointing professional librarians exclusively can, lead only to good results is shown in the case of Harnack, who took over direction of the collection in 1905 and supervised its transfer to the splendid new building.[17]

Althoff worked for organic cooperation among all libraries no less industriously than for the welfare of the Royal Library. To this end decree followed upon decree. In 1885 publication was begun in Berlin of yearly catalogues of German university publications.[18] and soon thereafter a catalogue of school program dissertations,[19] From 1892 on, the Berlin library printed lists of newly acquired titles, at first alone, then six years later in conjunction with all the Prussian university libraries.[20] An additional undertaking was the inventory of all the older books up to 1898 in an alphabetical union catalogue. The idea was not new: it had been aired already in several countries. In Germany it had emerged in the forties. Urged on by Althoff, Treitschke brought the matter to a head in an essay in the *Preussische Jahrbücher*. In the middle of the nineties the work began, and today it is complete in preliminary form. Since the first World

War and its consequences made impossible for the time being the printing of the catalogue, the Berlin Information Bureau (Auskunftsbüro Deutscher Bibliotheken) has assumed special importance.[21] It was opened in 1905 and developed into a center of bibliographical research. Finally, all these organizations became useful on a wide scale through the system of interlibrary loan (Deutscher Leihverkehr), which since 1892 has bound German libraries to one another in ever-widening scope.

The other events of Althoff's regime—the creation of a German music collection in Berlin and the catalogue of incunabula[22]—can only be mentioned in passing. From them all emanates the same spirit. Basically it is Leibniz's plan of organization made real by Althoff and his circle with modern methods and adapted to modern needs.

Chapter IX.
From The Nineteenth To The Mid-Twentieth Century

The period from the nineteenth through the mid-twentieth century witnessed numerous developments in the history of libraries, so that the focus in this chapter will primarily concentrate on areas of particular importance: national and scholarly libraries and the evolution of the public library up to the middle of the 20th century.

Many of the great libraries of Europe now look back upon a long past through which they had developed distinctive characteristics. But in the course of this historic development they have also fallen into groups, usually defined by national boundaries, and these groups possess traits whose explanation can be found in the history of their respective nations. The history of the great national libraries of France and Great Britain has already been presented. They have gone along their accustomed paths steadily, with some interruptions by wars and economic crises, but in essential continuity with their past.[1] These libraries were joined by a third, the Library of Congress, which took a place among the leading national libraries of the world.

Founded in 1800, the Library of Congress grew rather slowly for the first century of its existence.[2] Thomas Jefferson took a keen interest in the library from the start; in fact its purchases during the first decade were made largely according to his recommendations. In 1814, when the invading British army set fire to Washington, the Library was completely destroyed. Shortly thereafter, Jefferson offered to Congress his distinguished personal collection, which became the nucleus of the new library. Two subsequent fires in 1825 and 1851 wrought no small havoc upon the collections, but their growth went forward steadily. In 1897, when the books were moved into a magnificent new building, there were some 800,000 printed volumes and 200,000 pamphlets. Transfer to the Library of Congress of the Registry of Copyright in 1870 had appreciably accelerated its growth.

*Figure 36: Library of Congress – 1890s. From an engraving
by Paul Pelz and Johann Schmitmeyer.*

In 1899 Herbert Putnam, then librarian of the Boston Public Library, was appointed Librarian of Congress. His administration was truly epoch-making.[3] By the time of his retirement in 1939 the library had grown to some 6,000,000 volumes, and it had become necessary to build a gigantic annex capable of housing over 7,000,000 volumes in addition to reading rooms and work-space for many of the library's processing operations. But physical growth merely reflects the expanding influence of the library, for it has become a center of national culture, and in its encouragement of scholarship and the arts has developed into a kind of national university. Always strong in Americana, the library built up special fields such as Slavic and Oriental languages, acquired outstanding collections of music, maps, and prints, and added impressively to its manuscript holdings. It is impossible to survey here in a brief space the many diverse highlights of its collections,[4] but reference can be made to the Hispanic literature and history collections, for example.

In 1927 a generous endowment made it possible to create the Hispanic Foundation, and the following year another gift provided for a consultant in Hispanic literature. A beautiful Hispanic Reading Room was created, and the work of the foundation centered in one section of the building.

The Hispanic Foundation represents the archetype of a scholarly service that has evolved in a number of fields. The library added to its permanent staff a group of specialists holding endowed chairs and a further group of consultants and fellows, some of the latter being in residence for short terms. Thus the special collections were under constant scrutiny,

Figure 37: Reading Room – Library of Congress, circa 1890s.

Figure 38: Grand Stairway – Library of Congress, circa 1890s.

and in many of the leading fields of learning users of the library had expert advice.

To add to these notable advances in book-holdings and personnel the Library of Congress steadily expanded a number of special services which it fulfilled as a national institution. Of these perhaps the most widely influential was distribution of printed catalogue cards. Over 100 libraries in the United States and other countries had received depository sets; many of these libraries substituted the printed catalogue and its supplements. The possibility of purchasing catalogue cards prepared by experts revolutionized the cataloguing procedures of American libraries, large and small. A number of the

Figure 39: Hallway – Library of Congress, circa 1890s.

larger reference libraries contributed copy for certain classes of books, thus putting cataloguing in the United States to some extent on a cooperative basis and presenting recurrent inducements to standardize cataloguing practices. With the printing of *A Catalog of Books Represented by Library of Congress Printed Cards Issued to July 31, 1942,* and the supplements,[5] libraries throughout the world had a most helpful bibliographical aid. *Subject Headings Used in the Dictionary Catalogs of The Library of Congress* (5th ed., Washington, 1948), with its cumulative supplements, provided an outstanding cataloguing tool. The library also published a large number of bibliographies, some highly specialized and exhibiting accomplished scholarship. The monthly checklist of state documents compiled by the Documents Division became especially useful.

Another service which grew in importance each year was the Union Catalog, in which some 14,000 cards had been filed by 1946: Working closely with the Union Catalog was the Photo duplication Service, which became more and more active with the rapid development of methods of photo-duplication. The Union Catalog aimed to provide a national catalog of library holdings with references to library locations of the works listed.

Very much more might be said about other outstanding activities of the Library of Congress such as its promotion of music through the Coolidge and Whittall Foundations, but here it may be enough to close with mention of Dr. Putnam's successors. Archibald MacLeish, like Adolf von Harnack, was not a trained librarian, but he quickly acquired a firm grasp of technical problems, while his acknowledged eminence as a literary figure gave the library added impetus as a center of national culture. His impact upon the technical operations of the library is described in his own essay, "The Reorganization of the Library of Congress, 1939-44,"[6] but even more important than organizational reforms were the vision and spirit which he brought with him and infused into the library and its staff. MacLeish was wise enough to form an advisory committee of the leading librarians of the day, which assisted him and the library greatly. MacLeish's successor, Luther Evans, was distinguished by inexhaustible energy and the vast scope of his interests. Within the first year or two of his tenure he put the Library of Congress more firmly at the head of the American library profession than ever before. Some idea of this leadership can be gleaned from the *Annual Reports* from 1945 to 1947.

Other collections of national significance in Washington, D.C. are: the National Library of Medicine and the National Library of Agriculture, both the largest libraries of their kind. The National Archives is another collection of national significance in the nation's capital. Together with the Library of Congress, they contribute to making the constellation of collections in Washington, D.C. the greatest central repository of library materials in the world.

Apart from these collections there are, of course, many research libraries scattered through the United States and Canada. Some are private institutions like the Huntington Library in California. Others are public libraries like the New York Public Library, which, with some 4,500,000 volumes (in 1947), is one of the greatest research libraries in the world. The majority, however, are university libraries. A few have long histories and great collections. The Harvard University Library, for example, contained just under 5,000,000 volumes; and the Yale University Library, dating from 1701, owned over 3,600,000 volumes by mid twentieth-century. But many were fairly young. This was particularly true in the Midwest, where collections to be reckoned with, sometimes running to a million volumes or more, were built up in less than a century. It is characteristic of all these institutions, whatever their structure and financial support, that they were liberally open to any serious student with little formality.

The continuing influence of a regional and particularistic forces has long been characteristic of Germany. Political unification of the numerous small states and principalities comparatively late, and even the intense and comprehensive measures of unification undertaken by the Third Reich did not obliterate differences of tradition and practice rooted deep in the history of institutions. In the individual states of Germany there were state, provincial, and university libraries quite dissimilar in structure. Along with these were to be found municipal libraries in each of which a distinctive local character persists. Taking pre-war statistics, Berlin far surpassed any other German city in book-holdings. The Prussian State Library alone contained nearly 3,000,000 volumes,[7] and the other Berlin libraries, including those of the numerous government agencies, together had about 8,000,000 volumes. But the Bavarian State Library at Munich had over 2,000,000 volumes, and the annexation of Austria acquired temporarily for Germany two very large institutions with over a million volumes—the Vienna National Library and the Vienna University Library. Moreover Germany had five state and municipal libraries with about a million volumes, and five with about a half a million volumes. The war, hence, has wrought havoc upon practically all the great libraries of Germany.[8]

For years efforts to create a German national library were frustrated by the problem of depository copies. In 1848 the publisher Hahn of Hanover presented his stock of publications to the Frankfurt Parliament as the nucleus of a national library. About forty colleagues followed his example, and a librarian was appointed to take charge. Several years later the books of this new institution were removed to the Germanic Museum at Nürnberg. Not until after the empire was established did Hahn's plan revive. Then the publisher Brockhaus took it up; Treitschke discussed it in the *Preussische Jahrbücher*, and the librarians Dziatzko, Hartwig, and Wilmanns addressed a memorandum to the Ministry of Education. Among other things the plan at this time called for building up the royal Library at Berlin into a great national institution. But now, when political conditions were not unfavorable, the publishers balked at being called upon by a law of the Reich to deposit copies of their books. Opposition came also from special groups: for example, not long afterwards several attempts were made to establish a separate Catholic central library.

Despite all obstacles the project did not bog down. For this credit is due first and foremost to Althoff, who saw in its consummation the crowning of his efforts in behalf of libraries. To him can be traced the proposal to create a separate library of the Association of German Publishers and Book-dealers (Börsenverein der Deutschen Buchhändler) and he did not insist that it should be located in Berlin. In 1912 an agreement was signed by the State of Saxony, the City of Leipzig, and the Börsenverein creating the Deutsche Bücherei. According to its statutes the function of the Deutsche Bücherei is "beginning with January 1, 1913 to collect all literature which appears in German and in foreign languages within Germany, to preserve it, to make it available, and to record it by scientific principles." Heroic efforts were exerted to induce all publishers, associations, official bodies, and those who issued works outside the trade to submit deposit copies to the Deutsche Bücherei. By 1916 a high degree of success had been achieved.

Not only did the Deutsche Bücherei serve as a German book archive; it also performed extensive reference services, maintained public reading rooms, and lent books when they could not be obtained from another German library. By far its most important function aside from collecting was its bibliographical publishing. In 1921 it began to issue three trade bibliographies—a daily and a weekly list of new books and a list of new periodical and serial publications. The preparation of a monthly list of official publications began in 1928. The greatest bibliographical undertaking was the *Deutsche Nationalbibliographie*, begun in 1931. Four years later the Deutsche Bücherei took over publication of the *Jahresverzeichnis der deutschen Hochschulschriften*, which was assigned to it by the Ministry for Science, Education, and Popular Enlightenment. Urged on by the same ministry, in 1937 the Deutsche Bücherei entered upon a project that had been desired since 1920—centralized cataloguing. Special library issues of the trade bibliography have been printed on one side of the sheet for some years and used by some 200 libraries; in 1937 printed cards began to appear which were used by over 150 libraries.[9]

Severe economic stringency, particularly the post-war inflation of the early twenties, seriously threatened the very existence of the Deutsche Bücherei: indeed in 1920 it was even proposed to close the institution. But support rallied around the library from all sides. The most encouraging move came from the national government, which recognized the library as an institution of national significance and became a regular contributor to its income. The seizure of power by the National Socialists gradually led to the assumption by the Third Reich of the leading role in the control of the library. Revision of the copyright laws of the several German states in 1935 removed the deposit of copies from the status of voluntary contribution and achieved in effect a national law of legal deposit. In 1940 a government decree changed the legal basis of the library, making it a public institution under the supervision of the Minister of National Enlightenment and Propaganda. The Deutsche Bücherei came through the war with only slight damage; of all the major libraries in Germany, it was in the best position to carry on its normal functions in the postwar period.

In contrast to Germany, France has long been considered the example *par excellence* of strong central government and this tendency is reflected in the organization of

French library service.[10] The Bibliothèque Nationale is by far the largest library in the country, with about 4,500,000 volumes by mid 20th century. The remaining libraries of Paris together had some 8,000,000. Administratively, furthermore, several of the more important Parisian libraries, such as the Arsenal, the Sainte Geneviève, and the Mazarine are under the aegis of the Bibliothèque Nationale. The National and University Library of Strasbourg (Bibliothèque Nationale et Universitaire de Strasbourg) possessed a fine collection of 1,700,000 volumes, of which some 500,000 were lost during the war.[11] Aside from all these there are only three other libraries in France which approach or exceed 500,000 volumes. As was pointed out in the previous chapter, the Revolution inaugurated a movement toward uniformity which affected chiefly the large state libraries and university libraries. The Ministry of Education, by virtue of a series of decrees over a long span of years, has produced a good deal of uniformity in staff and administration. Even municipal libraries, though left to local authority, are subject to ministerial supervision.[12] What such impressive organization can accomplish is shown by the printing of the *Catalogue général des manuscrits des bibliothèques publiques de France* which, began in 1885. Germany, by contrast, had to labor for some forty years before similar nationwide undertakings such as the *German Union Catalogue* could reach the printing stage.

In its library organization Italy holds a position half-way, as it were, between France and Germany. It has many great old collections which grew up individually over a long period. With the political unification of Italy these libraries were taken under the wing of the new kingdom and a high degree of uniformity was introduced into their organization, a process which was continued and perhaps intensified under the Fascist regime.

There are thirty-two state libraries in Italy, many of them formerly old and famous private libraries whose history we have already traced.[13] Of these, two (at Florence and Rome) are national central libraries entitled to a copy of every book published in the republic. The National Central Library at Florence (Biblioteca Nazionale Centrale di Firenze), formerly the Magliabechi Library, is the largest in Italy, with over 2,500,000 volumes and pamphlets. Since 1886 it published the official national bibliography, the *Bollettino delle pubblicazioni italiane.* The Victor Emmanuel National Central Library (Biblioteca Nazionale Centrale Vittorio Emmanuele II) at Rome concentrates on collecting foreign books, and publishes a list of foreign publications acquired by Italian state libraries, the *Bollettino delle opere moderne straniere acquisitate delle biblioteche pubbliche governative del Regno d'Italia.* Five other libraries on the peninsula are designated "national" libraries; each is located in the chief city of a province, and exercises general supervision over the libraries of the province. There are still many fine private libraries in Italy and a large number of church libraries, headed by the two great papal institutions, the Ambrosian Library at Milan and the Vatican Library.

Italy can boast of one of the great libraries of the world in the Vatican. After a period of relative quiescence this library took a new lease on life late in the nineteenth century and transformed itself into one of the most progressive and efficiently administered libraries in Europe. This progress was accomplished under the leadership of a succession of extraordinarily brilliant directors; Father (later Cardinal) Franz Ehrle, 1895-1913; Mgr. Achille Ratti, 1913-1922 (before this he had been librarian of the Ambrosian, and later became Pope Pius XI); Mgr. (later Cardinal) Giovanni Mercati, 1922-1936; and the present incumbent, Mgr. Anselmo Albareda; in addition, Cardinal Eugene Tisserant was Curator of Oriental Manuscripts from 1908-1930, and Acting Director from 1930-1936. Many notable collections were acquired by the Vatican Library in the past few decades: among them might be mentioned the collections of the Borghese and Barberini families, the Chigi Library, the Caetani Archives, and many others of high distinction. Numerous improvements in buildings and administration, begun under Father Ehrle, culminated in the grandiose reorganization effected under the sponsorship of Pius XI. In 1888, under Leo XIII, the Vatican Library had been thrown open to the public, a reference room created, and added space provided for readers. As new collections streamed in with the passing years, more space was urgently needed. Various make-shifts only postponed the inevitable readjustments and enlargements which, begun in 1927 and completed in 1933, have greatly increased the book capacity, partly by use of Snead stacks, and provided excellent quarters for staff and readers.

The building program undertaken in 1927 coincided with a wholesale reorganization of the administrative procedures of the library, in particular with a notable reform of its cataloguing. After preliminary negotiations carried on in 1926 and 1927, a group of leading American librarians, headed by William Warner Bishop, librarian of the University of Michigan, and sponsored by the Carnegie Endowment for International Peace, arrived at the Vatican in February, 1928. In the meantime four members of the library staff had been sent to the United States to study American methods. As a result of the work of the visiting commission, a complete new cataloguing system was printed for books, very similar to the American system, was adopted. The Library of Congress made the Vatican Library one of its depositories for card sets, and the library, in turn, adopted Library of Congress printed cards in cataloguing its books. Cards were printed for books not represented by Library of Congress cards, and were sold to other libraries. A classified catalogue of Library of Congress was maintained. A manual of cataloguing rules based upon Library of Congress practice was published.[14] This manual, along with the successful demonstration of a dictionary catalogue in use, had some effect upon other European libraries. The Vatican Library retained its hereditary character as a great manuscript collection, and consequently close attention was paid to the cataloguing of manuscripts. A card index was decided upon as the most useful approach to the collection.[15]

The influence of the Vatican Library upon other libraries and upon the world of scholarship was strengthened not only by its cataloguing but also by publications of great scholarly value. An expansion of its scope was the creation of library school designed primarily to train personnel for ecclesiastical and parochial libraries. With all these activities the Vatican Library moved into the very front rank of European libraries.

Only brief notice can be taken here of other European nations. The Scandinavian countries had flourishing national libraries, and had given special effort to building public library service around their national libraries. One of the youngest European national libraries is the Swiss National Library at Bern. Founded in 1895, it grew quite rapidly, and had over 700,000 volumes (1947). In 1931 it formally opened a new building which was one of the leading examples of modern functional library architecture. New books are deposited by the great majority of Swiss publishers on a voluntary basis, in return for which the publisher receives a copy of the monthly bulletin of new books, *Das Schweizer Buch (Le livre Suisse)*, published by the library. Other current bibliographies were also issued, and a union catalogue listing the holdings of over a hundred Swiss libraries was maintained.[16]

In Russia the Leningrad Public Library, historically the great national library, made tremendous strides since the Revolution. The number of volumes just about trebled, partly as a result of government confiscation of private libraries. All modern improvements in library practice were eagerly investigated, and many adopted. For example, the library printed some 50,000 card sets each year and exchanged them with such diverse institutions as the Vatican Library and the Library of Congress. Two other developments may be pointed out. One was the Lenin Memorial Library in Moscow, for which a vast new modern building was completed, and which was one of the largest libraries in the world. The other was the great number of large collections constituting libraries of academies, institutes, and universities as well as regional and provincial libraries scattered over the vast expanse of the Soviet Union.

We have seen how one of the forces determining the development of libraries has been nationalism, how the character of a single library or of a group of libraries is conditioned by the size and organization of the social order to which it belongs. But there are even wider determining forces—the general historical conditions of an age, in the broadest sense of the term. The period from 1815 to the present has been characterized historically by nationalism. But there has been another movement which has swept across national boundaries and been united by common ties all over the world. If we wish to assign specific dates, we might say that the century beginning with 1848 has been the century of the common man. Enlargement of political franchise and spread of education have been paralleled by the development of the public library. Aside from formal education there has been what might be called general popularization of knowledge. In the United States the Lyceum movement and Chatauqua were really forms of the adult education movement which is so strong today. Similar activities are to be found in other countries. In this century one of the striking phenomena in the publishing world has been the success of popularizations of scientific and scholarly advances. Since it is the United States which made the most progress in this respect, the American scene will be surveyed before going on to Europe.

Limitless faith in education has grown to be part of the American idea. That acute observer, Alexis de Tocqueville, wrote in 1835: "In the United States the whole education of the people is directed toward politics."[17] Everyone, regardless of birth or position, should be educated to be a worthy citizen of what Münsterberg has called "ethical democracy." In this educational process the library acquired a place alongside the school. Much of the success of the American public library arises from the early realization that it must continue the educational work of the school and provide further opportunities for those whose formal schooling has ended. Consequently the library aims to broaden the interests of its readers, to help them with their vocational problems, and to supply good recreational reading. Every effort was made to attract all classes of people, to remove all hindrances, and thus to make the widest possible use of books. Something of the enthusiasm and technique of American business slipped into American library practice: the library tried to "sell" the worth-whileness of its wares to the user. Publicity devices such as exhibitions, newspaper articles, and radio broadcasts were actively exploited, and suggestions from the public welcomed. The library often sponsored lectures or musical programs, and thus took its place as the cultural and intellectual center of the city. These attempts to improve educational facilities in the widest sense caused the American public library to be referred to as "the people's university."

But the so-called American idea itself was something which developed in the eighteenth century and became articulate with the Revolution; then there arose the vast problem of implementing the idea by practical measures. Faith in education was but a corollary of the notion of the indefinite perfectibility of man, a leading idea of the

Enlightenment which found its way via the French *philosophes* into the mental furniture of such men as Franklin and Jefferson. Achievement of a comprehensive educational system took years. The earliest colonial tradition was to provide schooling for the children of those who could afford it. The first American universities, such as Harvard, William and Mary, and Yale, were designed essentially to train new members of the ministry. Only gradually was free education provided by the community for those children whose parents could not afford to furnish it at their own expense, and even then these common schools smacked of charity and were often not attended by children of more prosperous families. Not until the middle of the nineteenth century did the concept of free common schools for all children gain ascendancy, and the first state law making education compulsory was not passed until 1852.

The typical American public library as we now know it, a free, tax-supported institution, likewise did not come into being until the middle of the nineteenth century.[18] In the two hundred years preceding it, several other kinds of libraries supplied reading matter to the public. We shall pass over private libraries and early college libraries as not being really public. Among the earliest public libraries where those established in some of the southern states, notably Maryland, Virginia, and the Carolinas, by the Rev. Thomas Bray, the eminent divine and missionary. There were also some parish libraries in existence in northern states. Dr. Bray, entrusted with supervision of Anglican churches in Maryland, saw that one of the conditions which would attract young clergymen of ability to the colony was assurance of having books at their disposal. Consequently he set about providing parish libraries "for the clergy and gentry." The basic collection for these libraries was carefully supervised by Dr. Bray, catalogues were drawn up, and provisions made for lending books.[19]

The next important step was instigated by no less a personage than Benjamin Franklin. This was the organization in 1731 of the first subscription library in America, the Free Library Company of Philadelphia. The next hundred years saw the founding of similar libraries in many other cities, the best known being the Boston Athenaeum, the New York Society Library, and the Charleston (S.C.) Library Society. Some of the subscription libraries have retained their independence to the present day. A larger number, however, were either forced out of existence by the subsequent emergence of public libraries, or evolved into public libraries.

Membership in a subscription library, however, was possible only for those of better-than-average means, and even so it was not long before many subscription libraries found it expedient to admit readers on the basis of an annual subscription without enforcing the condition of an initial purchase of shares. Meanwhile other strata of the populace began to organize libraries to serve their needs. The first decades of the nineteenth century saw the beginnings of mechanics' and mercantile libraries, the desirability and general character of which had already been outlined by Franklin. These libraries were motivated primarily by the needs of young men—artisans, mechanics, clerks—to improve themselves in their vocations and to spend their leisure to good advantage: in this way they hoped to acquire broader culture and to rise in their careers.

None of these libraries was yet a public library in the present connotation of the term. The bridge between the "social" libraries we have been describing and the true public library was the school-district library. In 1835 the New York state legislature passed a law authorizing each school-district to lay a tax for the purchase of libraries. Subsequent legislature and grants of money enabled the school-district libraries to blossom rapidly. Other states imitated the system; by 1876 nineteen additional states had passed similar laws. But the school-district was not a practicable unit, and administrative difficulties and political abuses caused the New York school-district library movement to pass its peak and start downhill within twenty years. A similar fate befell these libraries in other states. A relic of the school-district movement remains today in about half a dozen states, with forty cities having public libraries organized on the basis of the school-district as the governmental unit, and even here, as Joeckel has been able to show, the looser the connection between school and library, the better the library service.[20] The school-district movement in the two decades after 1835 had acted nevertheless as an entering wedge: taxes had been authorized by state legislatures for the support of public libraries.

A true public library, supported by public taxation but still without a state enabling act, was established by the town of Peterborough, New Hampshire, in 1833. To the state of New Hampshire also goes credit for having passed the first general library law in 1849. But leadership in the movement was soon taken over by the state of Massachusetts and its capital city, Boston. During the first half of the nineteenth century some sixty laws relating to libraries had been passed by Massachusetts. In 1848 the city of Boston was authorized to establish a tax-supported public library. In 1851 a general law extended the privilege to other towns throughout the state. At first limits were set to tax increases for library purposes, but these were later abolished. Since 1890 the state has provided funds for the promotion of libraries and has created a library commission which has served as a model for other states. In 1939 Massachusetts had 405 public libraries, 77 of them in communities with less than 1,000 inhabitants.

There had been some lively interest in a public library in Boston for some time before the legislative act made it possible to go ahead with its creation. One of its most enthusiastic proponents was the Harvard professor, George Ticknor, who had studied at Göttingen in 1815 and been profoundly impressed by the richness and liberality of the university library. During the years when the proposal to establish the library was being pushed, Ticknor wrote in one of his letters: "The public library should come in at the end of our system of free instruction, and be fitted to continue and increase the effects of that system by the self-culture that results from reading"—-this in contrast to Prussia, where one had no such opportunity after leaving school. Ticknor's program, supported by a group of eminent Bostonians, became realized in 1854 with the opening of the Boston Public Library. The library has grown steadily, has twice acquired a new building, has established branch libraries and deposit stations throughout the city, and in 1939 possessed about 1,750,000 volumes, including some splendid special collections.

The greatest of American public libraries, the New York Public Library, developed out of three large endowments. In 1848 the German-American merchant prince, John Jacob Astor, left $400,000 for the purpose of founding a library, which was incorporated in 1849. Its director, Joseph Green Cogswell, once a fellow-student of Ticknor's at Göttingen, had spent some years before Astor's death buying books for the library on Astor's commission. A second independent foundation, established in 1870, was the Lenox Foundation, containing a distinguished collection. The will of Samuel J. Tilden, a prominent citizen and man of affairs, who died in 1886, left a large bequest to be used for establishing and maintaining a free public library in New York City, but litigation delayed execution of the will for some years. These three separate endowments were

Figure 40: Public Library, Boston, Mass.

merged in 1895. In 1896 a great organizer, John Shaw Billings, became Director of the New York Public Library.[21] Under his leadership, and speeded by a munificent gift in 1901 from Andrew Carnegie, which created 65 branches at one stroke, there took place a merger of a number of circulating libraries, which had been operating independently, with the New York Public Library. The library had a Reference Department with a massive building in the center of the city containing a superb collection of some 3,000,000 volumes and a Circulation Department with about 1,500,000 volumes and 60-odd branches.

In general the progress of the American public library movement was slow until the last quarter of the nineteenth century. The year 1876—something of a wonder year in American cultural history—witnessed a number of developments which measurably accelerated the movement. In that year the American Library Association was founded, and the first number of the *Library Journal* appeared. The *American Catalogue* and the special report of the United States Bureau of Education on public libraries were published. The Library Bureau was established to supply libraries with the various kinds of equipment they require, Melvil Dewey published the first edition of his *Decimal Classification* and took a leading part in creating the American Library Association. From this year on Dewy's influence in the library world was strong up to the end of the century. It was he who headed the first library school in the United States, opened in 1887. Since that time a number of library schools have been founded, concerning which we shall have more to say later.

Certain characteristics and traditional services came to be recognized as part of the essence of the American public library of the mid-twentieth century. These we shall try to outline, with the one precautionary reservation that what is being portrayed is a type and that variations from this type were very great among American public libraries. In general a large public library had all the features mentioned, and more,[22] whereas the smaller libraries did not provide all these services. A typical, well-organized public library, then was open long hours, usually well into the evening and often on Sundays. An open stack, giving readers direct access to the books, was one of the important American contributions to public library practice. In addition, book lists showing new accessions are often published, and a readers' advisory service is maintained. Efforts were made to display the library's facilities in connection with contemporary problems such as proposed legislation, or political and social questions, or with historic occasions such as national holidays. Various other publicity devices already mentioned were freely used. Not infrequently there would be a lecture room in the library building. In addition to circulating books practically all American libraries consider it part of their function to maintain reference service which will provide information with speed and efficiency. This service was a kind of bridge between public and scholarly libraries in the United States, for as a public library grows in size and its reference service expands, it took on some of the functions performed by university and special research libraries. A fast developing service, of which the Library of Congress became the center, was provision of books for the blind.

Among the finest activities of American public libraries were their provisions for children. Separate rooms were opened with collections of juvenile literature graded according to age, and librarians paid much attention to the psychology of children and their use of books. Children's librarians worked closely with schools, sending special collections to the classroom on loan, and in return teachers encouraged and instructed children, beginning in the lowest grades, in the use of the library. Here was a close and fruitful relation between school and library operating to lay a firm foundation for the great educational achievement envisioned in the American idea.

American public libraries owe their existence, for the most part, to local initiative abetted by private philanthropy. The greatest individual benefactor of public libraries, Andrew Carnegie, who gave over $40,000,000 for public library buildings, insisted on preserving local responsibility by making his grants contingent upon the guarantee of

Figure 41: Public Library, Fargo, North Dakota.

minimal support of the library by the community. Carnegie's gifts to the public libraries were much more extensive, however, elsewhere. He established libraries in Britain, the Dominions, and the Colonies as well. Under these conditions, and considering also the differences in geography, economic resources, date of settlement, and other cultural factors throughout this vast and various continent, it is not surprising that the quality of library service should vary widely from place to place. Particularly inadequate were services to rural communities which fall outside the governmental limits of municipalities. Following the example set by Massachusetts, state library commissions were created, and in a number of states such as New York, Ohio, Indiana, and particularly California, with its system of free county libraries, much was done to eliminate the condition. But the depression of the thirties and social analyses which came in its wake forced a painful awakening to the fact that some forty million people in the United States were still without library service.

Much of this was due to the complex and irrational governmental structure of the American public library, which put artificial obstacles in the way of regional library service. To the problem C.B. Joeckel devoted a masterly study, and one of his suggestions, library service on the basis of municipal trading areas, may be a practicable solu-

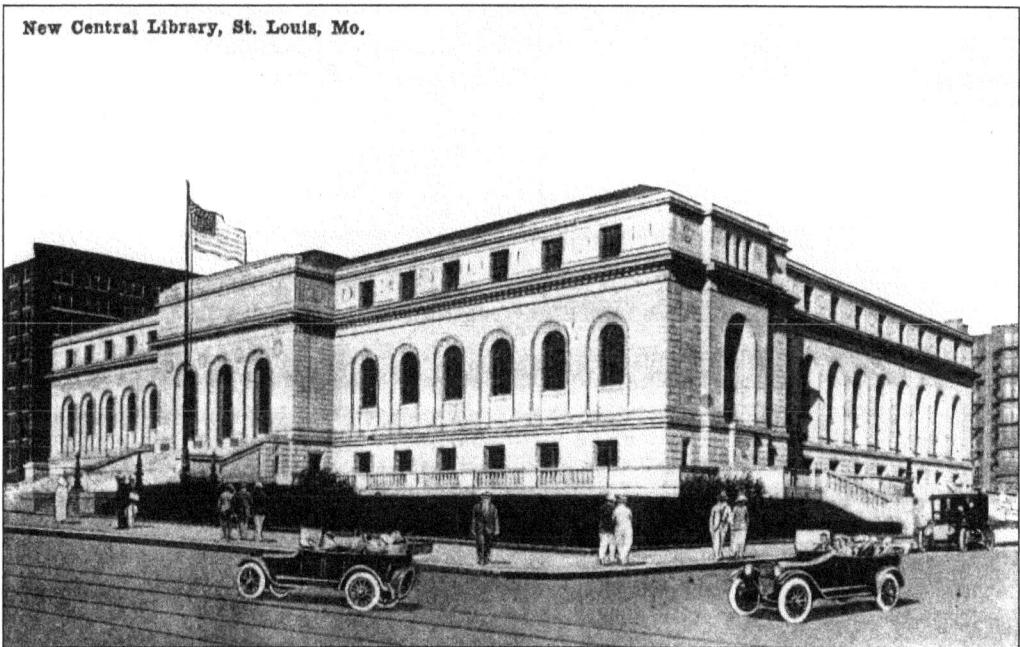

New Central Library, St. Louis, Mo.

Figure 42: New Central Library, St. Louis, Missouri

tion, though it would involve difficulties in political, legislative, and administrative readjustment. Many of the areas were so poor—and were furthermore sections of larger areas, such as counties or states, suffering from financial distress—that nothing short of federal subsidy similar to that advanced for agricultural extension and vocational education would be effective. The federal government was aware of this problem. In 1938 a Division of Library Service was created in the Office of Education. At any rate, experiments with regional library service made possible by new conditions, such as those in the Tennessee Valley, demonstrated what can be done by basing library service upon regions which have natural geographic and economic unity.

The British public library system showed marked likeness to the American in many respects, yet there are interesting differences. The average British public library was perhaps not so highly developed as its American counterpart: in particular, certain techniques such as library publicity have not been carried through so thoroughly because of differences of tradition. Other long-established American developments, for example county libraries and library schools, came fairly late to Great Britain. On the other hand, as will appear, planning for library service on a nationwide basis was carried farther in Great Britain than in the United States.

The question of priority and of influence in historical development cannot be fully answered.[23] That each country has influenced the other continuously is hardly to be doubted. Aside from the constant traditional cultural interchange, there are such specific instances as the early affiliation of the American Library Association and the Library Association of the United Kingdom, and in general the parallel evolution of so many features of the institution in both countries. For example, open stack, Dewey Decimal Classification, and reference service was to be found in most British and American public libraries by mid-twentieth century. Most significant historically is the fact that the great initial impetus to the development of the public library system came at exactly the same time in both countries. Unquestionably we have here a case of the simultaneous operation of the same large social force, the Industrial Revolution with its attendant phenomena—emergence of large cities, growth of a laboring class needing improved technical education, enlargement of the franchise, and growing political consciousness of the people along with spread of education.

In Great Britain tentative attempts to provide public libraries quite similar to those in the United States can be traced back well over two centuries before the start of true public libraries. There were a few instances of libraries established by individual municipalities as early as the first decade of the seventeenth century. The Rev. Thomas Bray founded parish libraries in Great Britain also, some of them still being maintained. There were likewise the familiar subscription libraries (probably the most illustrious survivor of this type is the famous London Library, which was founded in 1841), and mechanics' libraries were especially numerous.

The parliamentary committee appointed in 1835 to inquire into the reform of the British Museum turned up a good deal of information concerning the state of other libraries throughout the realm. This marked the beginning of agitation for improved public libraries, in the forefront of which was Edward Edwards, whose efforts have entitled him to be considered the spiritual father of the English public library movement. He combined theoretical insight with practical ability and unceasing industry. In 1849, when a parliamentary committee began to take evidence concerning public libraries, Edwards played a leading role in supplying it. He worked closely with the chairman, William Ewart, who was to be found in the front rank of every fight for public education. Through Ewart, Edwards furnished the committee with detailed data he had been collecting for some years, and sponsored a number of general principles which eventually found their way into the committee's report. The account which Edwards has written of the public library movement in his country is still a classic.

In 1845 Parliament had passed a law empowering town councils to levy taxes for the purpose of establishing public museums. The town of Warrington had taken advantage of this law to establish a museum and a library. Now, in 1850, Parliament extended the taxing power of the town councils to the establishment of public libraries in boroughs of over 10,000 population. Further legislation in succeeding years culminated in the Public Libraries Act of 1892, providing that every urban district, should be a library district. Similar laws were passed for Scotland and Ireland about the same time. With some modifications, these are still the main library laws under which British libraries operate.[24]

The Library Act of 1850 was permissive: it still left the founding of libraries to local initiative. A few cities were quick to take advantage of the act and, as the years passed, more and more cities were added to their number. Yet, on the whole, progress was slow. Extension of school legislation in the seventies caused a quickening of tempo, as did also the founding of the Library Association in 1877. The Jubilee Year of Queen Victoria, 1887, was widely celebrated by the founding of libraries. But perhaps the most important impetus came from the benefactions of J. Passmore Edwards and of Andrew Carnegie, culminating in creation of the Carnegie United Kingdom Trust in 1913. The large industrial city of Manchester has played in England a role of analogous to that of Boston in the United States. Its public library was opened in 1852 and directed for six years by Edward Edwards in exemplary manner. To the present day it continues to be a leader among British public libraries. Metropolitan London, however, has always lagged behind, partly because of the complexity of its governmental structure.

Great Britain was ahead of the United States in at least one very important aspect of its public library system—nationwide coverage. Legally this can be accomplished with comparative ease. In the United States permissive measures for local library units had to be passed in each of the 48 states, which has meant a good deal of variety in library laws. In Great Britain, Parliament has been able from the beginning to pass laws providing for all the United Kingdom. This effects greater unity from the start. The First World War resulted in the necessity of economic reconstruction for the nation. Among the comprehensive measures for reconstruction was the Library Act of 1919, which removed hitherto obstructive limits to library taxation and created county library authorities.

The most important single factor making for nationwide coverage, however, was the development of the National Central Library. Chiefly as a result of demands made by educators, this was established in 1916 with a Carnegie grant as the Central Library for Students to act as a center of bibliographical information and as a central lending agency. It steadily expanded its functions, with constant support of the Carnegie United Kingdom Trust. In 1930 the name was changed to the National Central Library, and in 1937 it occupied new large, modern quarters. The National Central Library had vast influence in inducing library cooperation throughout Britain, as well as British cooperation with other countries. It affiliated with it a number of general and special libraries known as "outliers" which agree to lend books from their collections upon request. The university libraries too, after an abortive attempt at a cooperative system of their own, joined the National Central Library system. Regional bureaus were built up to act as intermediaries between the individual student and the National Central Library. It was thus possible for readers who wished a particular title to apply directly to the National Central Library (if they lived in one of the comparatively few British areas without library service) or to their public library, which, if it did not have the book applied to the regional bureau or, if there was no regional bureau, directly to the National Central Library. By means of union catalogues or other bibliographical aids either the regional bureau or the central library supplied the book, borrowing it, perhaps, from an affiliated library, or buying it if other methods fail. The service given by the national Central Library steadily expanded, and appreciation of its usefulness increased.

The economic depression of the thirties and the outbreak of the Second World War combined to bring the problem of nationwide library service to the fore. After the First World War study of this problem continued. In 1927 the *Report on Public Libraries* aroused considerable interest, but was rather indeterminate. It was followed in 1929-30 by the *Final Report* of the Royal Commission on National Museums and Galleries, which made recommendations for libraries. The McColvin report (1942),[25] which appeared during the war, analyzed the current state of affairs and made courageous and far-flung plans for the reorganization of British library service. The report faced square-ly the several inadequacies of present-day conditions and advanced detailed proposals to reconstruct the library system, if possible, in conjunction with changes in govern-ment and taxation, but if not, by a reform within the organization of library service itself which will be based upon geographic and economic regional units naturally suit-ed to provide the service.

In turning from American and British public libraries to those of continental Europe one must be careful to make certain definitions and distinctions. The term "public library" has come to be used for a library specifically and avowedly open for free general public use and financed by public taxation. Many "public" libraries in Europe were open to a fairly restricted clientele; a much smaller proportion than in the United States or Great Britain were publicly financed; and many of the libraries opened specially for popular reading charge small fees. Europe has always been outstanding for its large number of fine private libraries. In some measure the very existence of these private libraries militated against the establishment of public libraries, for often they have been liberally opened to the serious student. The public libraries of Europe fall into two large classes: the so-called "learned," "scholarly," or "scientific" libraries *(wis-senschaftliche Bibliotheken)* and the popular libraries *(Volksbibliotheken)*. In the first group are to be found the great reference libraries belonging to the nation, to univer-sities, to learned societies and institutions, and in some cases to private individuals who place little obstruction in the way of their use by the general public. These libraries we have already examined in some detail. The libraries of the second group vary consid-erably from country to country. In general the popular library serves primarily as a lending center. Little or no attempt was made to give reference service or gradually to build up a more serious background collection, a process which occurs naturally, so to speak, in British and American libraries. The popular library performed roughly the circulation functions of an American public library without offering to its users the adjoining potentialities for reference work or more serious study.

One exception to these generalizations must be made at the outset—the popular libraries of the Scandinavian countries. The development of the Scandinavian public library systems occurred at the turn of this century, when the American public library movement was already vigorous to exert strong influence. Norway was the first to adopt American methods such as open access, dictionary catalogue, and simplified charging systems. A number of Norwegians visited and studied in the United States and returned to pioneer in the transmission of American methods to their own country, from which these methods radiated to Denmark and Sweden. Two of the Norwegian pioneers, H. Tambs Lyche and Haakon Nyhuus, deserve special mention.[26] In Denmark the educator A.S. Steenberg, learning of American methods from a publication by the Austrian professor Eduard Reyer, enthusiastically propagandized for them. In all three Scandinavian countries the central government exercised careful supervision over libraries, largely by means of grants which reward good local library service. Technical aid in book-selection, purchase, and cataloguing was also given by the government. Nationwide coverage was very good; indeed Denmark was pointed to as ideal in this respect.

Germany has long been famous for its scholarly libraries and also for its many private libraries. But the development of popular libraries has been rather halting. Its first stage came between the wars of liberation (1813-15) and the middle of the century, which brought widespread social revolutions. Many small libraries belonging to associations of artisans and to educational association, and also a number of traveling libraries in rural districts sprang into existence. Worthy of note here is the work of the revenue official Karl Preusker, who propagandized for libraries for the community, brought about creation of a municipal library at Grossenhain in Saxony, and stimulated the Saxon Economic Society *(Sächsische Ökonomische Gesellschaft)* to establish village libraries.

Much of this progress failed to survive the mid-century revolution and the reaction which followed. A happy exception is to be seen in the public libraries of Berlin, which originated through the efforts of the historian Friedrich von Raumer, who, as Ranke says, "was on the side of every moment of his time that could be called progressive." Motivated by impressions of a trip to America, he founded the Association for Scientific Lectures *(Verein für wissenschaftliche Vorträge)* in 1841, and made over its large proceeds to the city of Berlin, so that in 1850 the first four popular libraries could be opened. After almost two decades of continuous support from the association, the city took over sole financial responsibility. In the 1890s there was a reorganization: the book-collections were brought up to date, funds increased, and more convenient hours of opening adopted. In 1907 a central library was created, and the organization of Berlin public service has been suggested as a type toward which other municipalities should tend.[27] Before the war the central scholarly library had some 350,000 volumes. Under its control were some 130 popular libraries and special reading rooms. These were scattered through the 120 administrative districts of Berlin and the director of the Berlin Municipal Library had final control on technical and cultural policies and practices.

Progress outside Berlin had to wait until after the Empire was founded. In the last decade of the nineteenth century the larger cities made considerable gains. Two individuals must be singled out as leaders in the movement: Constantin Nörrenberg, librarian at Kiel, who had become acquainted with American practices on a trip to the Chicago Exposition in 1896, and Eduard Reyer, a Viennese professor who had also traveled in the United States and England, and who created a noteworthy organization of popular libraries (the *Verein Zentralbibliothek*) in his homeland. One result of this awakening interest in popular libraries was the founding of a professional journal, the *Blätter für Volksbibliotheken und Lesehallen*, in 1900.[28] Several societies also served the cause well: the Society for Ethical Culture *(Gesellschaft für Ethische Kultur)*, with its establishment of public reading rooms, the Comenius Society *(Comenius-Gesellschaft)*, and the Society for the Spread of Popular Education *(Gesellschaft zur Verbreitung der Volksbildung)*, whose activities were especially beneficial for rural districts and small communities.

In agricultural districts several German states encouraged the creation of regional organizations with traveling libraries. Saxony and Württemberg were the first to provide modest state aid, and Prussia has a long history of state sponsorship. In the frontier regions specially strong efforts were made to provide books. In 1896 a Union of Upper Silesian Popular Libraries *(Verband Oberschlesischer Volksbibliotheken)* was founded, and by 1914 it had made appreciable progress. The Kaiser Wilhelm Library in Posen became the center for town and rural popular libraries in its region. It operated a traveling library and united the institutions of the whole province under one administration. After the First World War the Frontier Library Service *(Grenzbüchereidienst)* was founded to supply literature that would strengthen nationalist feeling among those in areas removed from German control or threatened with removal by plebiscite. This organization was most successful, and indeed the Grenzbücherdienst may be looked upon as a prototype for other organizations created by the Third Reich to reclaim for Germany large numbers of its former inhabitants and to enlist the loyalty of people of German ancestry throughout the world.[29]

When it had got well under way, the German popular library movement could be seen to be moving clearly in the direction of separating the popular library from the scholarly library. Its early proponents aimed not only at creating new libraries but at transforming those already in existence. They induced most of the older municipal libraries to abandon competition with state and other scholarly libraries and to adopt the aims and policies of the new popular Librarians *(Verband Deutscher Volkbibliothekare)*. However, there was some reversal of this tendency.[30] The feeling was fairly widespread in Germany that popular libraries suffice for small communities, and that large cities which could afford it should have both a scholarly municipal library and a popular library system, separately administered. (In a few large cities, such as Berlin, administration of the two has been combined.) For middle-sized cities, however, a central library system combining the two types was being adopted. A new kind of library, the so-called "Einheitsbibliothek,"[31] thus came into being. The widespread destruction of the war and consequent economic difficulties encouraged a trend in Germany to the consolidation of libraries, particularly in those large or middle-sized cities which had both municipal and university libraries.

In both France and Italy popular libraries were badly underdeveloped by comparison with other countries. While centralized administration resulting from the revolution worked to the progressive advantage of French scholarly libraries (university libraries having made notable advances in recent times) municipal libraries languished. France had a few noteworthy municipal libraries, but they resembled scholarly German libraries much more than the public library of a good-sized American or British city. There had been neither adequate local initiative nor sufficient encouragement by the central government to provide satisfactory free lending libraries in the majority of French cities and towns. Just when interest was heightening—partly through the example set by the American Library in Paris—the severe economic distress of the 1930's made it impossible to get anything done. In the reconstitution of France after the recent war, organization of flourishing public libraries presented a major challenge and a great opportunity.

After political unification Italy had to take the preliminary step of eliminating widespread illiteracy. The popular libraries which came into being were largely sponsored by partisan groups: there were religious libraries or working-men's libraries with their own particular bias and with mutual antagonism. After the turn of the century the most important popular libraries were maintained by societies whose object was to improve the lot of the workers. In 1917 a law was passed making it obligatory for every commune to maintain a library, but conformity with this law was lax. The Fascist government took steps to stimulate the public library movement. Two Italian library associations *(Associazione Italiana per le Biblioteche and Ente Nazionale per le Biblioteche Populari e Scholastiche)* were founded, and training courses for librarians were started.

Striking progress in developing public libraries was made in Soviet Russia. It was an integral part of determined efforts made by the government to eliminate the high rate of illiteracy which existed in 1917 and to raise the educational and cultural level of the people. The amazing growth and distribution of new libraries was made possible partly, as in France, by confiscation of rich private collections, and partly also by fundamental government reorganization which provided an administrative basis for nationwide library service.

The most obvious evidence of this activity was the existence of so many large libraries. Spread throughout the expanse of the Union were many collections of hundreds of thousands—and sometimes a million or more—volumes which came into existence after the Revolution. Each of the constituent republics had a large and flourishing state library, and many municipal and regional libraries were of impressive proportions. The two greatest libraries in Russia were the Leningrad Public Library, which has a long and illustrious history, and the Lenin Memorial Library in Moscow, which had a capacity of about 10,000,000 volumes. Both these libraries numbered about 7,000,000 volumes by mid-20th century. Some idea of the size of state libraries can be gained from the Kharkov State Library, with over 1,000,000 volumes and the White Russian State Library at Minsk, with over 1,500,000 volumes.[32] Then there are university, school, and military libraries with sizable collections.[33] In addition, many institutions or associations had large libraries. By far the most important of these was the library of the Academy of Sciences, which, with its branches in Moscow and Leningrad combined contained some 7,000,000 volumes. The government provided for building up the most important of these large libraries by granting deposit privileges to a number of them throughout the union. Part of their growth was attributable to the large number of books published in Russia, which just before the war exceeded the combined production of the United States and Germany in one year.

Throughout Russia there was the familiar European distinction between scholarly and popular libraries. But Russian librarians contend, probably with some justice, that the difference was merely one of function. Large scholarly libraries maintained close contacts with popular (or, as they are called, mass) libraries, either by administering them as branches or by exercising what was called patronage—that is, providing advice and supervision. The collections of scholarly libraries were drawn upon heavily and regularly. Popular, or mass, libraries were exceedingly numerous, and were to be found scattered through municipal districts and in factories and workers' clubs and dormitories. Regional service for rural districts was supervised generally by the large state libraries. In setting up a system to provide library service for its far-flung peoples, the Soviet government solicited the advice of Harriet Eddy, formerly county library organizer in California, and sent one of its own librarians to the United States to study current practices.

In general Russian libraries were influenced more by American than European libraries. The Dewey Decimal Classification was widely used. Some of the larger libraries adopted the Brussels Expansion, and a few used the Library of Congress classification. A Marxist library classification was also worked out. Anglo-American cataloguing practice, with some natural modifications, was followed, and the Central Book

Chamber in Moscow did central cataloguing, issuing card-sets to Russian libraries. Open access was infrequent, but there was a tendency to adopt it more widely.

Bibliographical work of good quality was done in Russia. In addition to numerous national and special bibliographies prepared by the Central Book Chamber and the Leningrad Public Library,[34] all libraries paid a great deal of attention to promoting reading by preparing lists, and much work was done with individual readers, like that carried on at Leipzig under the leadership of Walter Hofmann. Taken all in all, the picture presented by Russian libraries was one of vigorous growth.

Chapter X. General Problems And Developments

L ooking back over the history of libraries we find certain problems with which all libraries are faced in any given historical period. Partly these are produced by the general historical climate, and partly they arise out of the evolution of the library. This chapter deals with general problems and developments faced by libraries up through the mid-20th century.

One of the gravest of these was space. Only a little more than a century after printing was been invented, Leibniz said: "If the world goes on this way for a thousand years and as many books are written as today, I am afraid that whole cities will be made up of libraries."[1] Two centuries later we find a similar flight of the imagination in America: the libraries of Cambridge (that is, of Harvard University) were to grow toward Boston, those of Boston toward Cambridge, until in the intervening space everything was to be submerged and drowned out in a sea of books. How serious the problem is can be appreciated from the fact that since 1876 large research libraries in America have approximately doubled in size each twenty years.[2] Since the adoption of steel stacks, which made it possible to use space more efficiently in storing books, was been no important architectural innovation: architectural improvements have been confined to attempts to do away with space-wasting monumental structures and to plan functional buildings.[3] But even relatively satisfactory buildings erected in this century were crammed to capacity with constantly growing collections. This made it necessary to examine the implications of future growth and to reconsider the principles governing storage and preservation of printed materials.

It has long been generally recognized that the use of books in libraries varies widely, that a few books are intensively used, some frequently, some occasionally, and a considerable proportion very rarely.[4] There were radical proposals to divide large collections into living and dead parts and to weed out the latter by discarding or selling volumes periodically. A more carefully thought- out proposal was made by President Eliot of Harvard in 1902: storage of little-used books in a separate place where they could be shelved by size, two or three deep, and thus inexpensively preserved apart from the central collection. Similar proposals for depositories outside large cities were advanced in America, Italy, and Germany. In 1931 the Association of German Librarians aired the whole question of storing so-called "dead" literature, but no practical steps were taken.[5] Meanwhile, however, several large libraries were adopting measures of this kind. In 1906 the British Museum built a special depository for newspapers at Hendon, a London suburb. By 1921 the building was full, and in 1932 it was enlarged and reopened as the Newspaper Library at Colindale.[6] The New York Public Library acquired an empty commercial loft about a mile from its central building in 1933 and fitted it out as a storehouse. All its newspaper files were moved to the storehouse, along with other bulky and little-used materials. In 1932-1934 the Bibliothèque Nationale constructed an annex for newspapers and journals at Versailles. All these measures gave genuine relief, but this relief was admittedly only temporary.

A more direct attack on the problem, stemming from President Eliot's proposals, was made in Boston. Here twelve research libraries—among them the two largest in the metropolitan area, the Harvard University Library and the Boston Public Library—joined to form a corporation which controls a recently constructed, inexpensive block building with a small reading room, but with the greatest part of its space given over to shelves for about 1,000,000 volumes. Since storage was the main objective, the height of the stack level was increased and the width of the aisles decreased. Space could be rented in any library, which used its own space as it sees fit.[7] By 1947 the Harvard University Library had moved over 200,000 volumes into the New England Deposit Library. Similar depositories are being planned by other large libraries.

New developments and new problems in classification and cataloguing were not lacking. During the Enlightenment tendencies in classification and cataloguing which had been developing for years came, as it were, to maturity. One school of librarians acquired a passion for classification and insisted that books on the shelf ought to be arranged to parallel the classed catalogue. This theory still had its adherents; indeed one librarian writes: "The German view is definitely that the arrangement of the catalog is the primary factor to which the arrangement of the books on the shelves must then be adapted, in so far as the library in question provides for classified or systematic shelving."[8] The last qualifying phrase is significant, however. Even during the Enlightenment, other librarians contended that consideration of space and physical convenience ought to determine the way in which books were shelved. In Europe faith in classification was gradually undermined. The great-hall structure, which united all the library's books into a kind of intellectual cosmos, disappeared, and with the separation of reading rooms and stack, which meant that the shelves were no longer open to readers in many research libraries, one of the incentives was removed. We have seen how in the early nineteenth century new systems of shelving books were adopted, notably at the Bibliothèque Nationale. Many European libraries, especially within Germany, divided their books into a few large groups within which they are arranged by size, and then in accession order. Subject catalogues have been started to accompany such changes, and in many libraries the classed catalogue, if not displaced, has came to be primarily a tool for staff use. [9]

In America, where access to the shelves was common, even in large research libraries, much effort was expended upon classification. The Dewey Decimal Classification, first published in 1876, and was used by the great majority of American public libraries, and also by some research libraries. College and research libraries, however, have shown a tendency to abandon the Dewey Classification as their collections grow beyond 100,000 volumes. A few large libraries in Europe have adopted the Universal Decimal Classification, an expansion of the Dewey scheme prepared by the International Federation for Documentation, but this was used less for library classification than for scientific documentation. In the United States another great scheme of classification was developed for the collections of the Library of Congress. The schedules have been printed, and there was a noticeable trend among college and research libraries toward adoption of the Library of Congress scheme. Printing of both Dewey and Library of Congress class numbers on Library of Congress catalogue cards was an added inducement to use one of the two schemes which have became more or less standard in America.

In cataloguing, the great development of the past fifty years was the emergence of the dictionary catalogue in English-speaking countries, and also in a few European libraries. Here America led the way. Printing of cards by the Library of Congress and their use by other libraries produced in American catalogues a greater degree of uniformity than could be found in any other country. Subject cataloguing was unified by the printing of Library of Congress guides (of which the fifth edition was published in 1948) and of guides sponsored by the H.W. Wilson Co. primarily for small libraries, but in close correlation with Library of Congress practice.

Serious thought was given to general cataloguing policies, especially to the cost of cataloguing. Publication of the Anglo-American code in 1908 was a milestone in cataloguing history, and produced highly beneficial results in raising the quality and unifying the practices of cataloguing in American and British libraries.[10] Gradually, over a period of forty years, supplementary rules mushroomed in the catalogue departments of individual libraries. This was particularly so in large libraries, of which the Library of Congress was perhaps the best example. At the same time the cost of cataloguing mounted alarmingly. Publication of a preliminary edition of the revised American Library Association code provided the occasion for American librarians to re-examine their policies.[11] A movement toward simplification in cataloguing gained strength, and impetus was lent by the Library of Congress adoption of simplified rules.[12]

Segregation of ephemeral and little-used material, which reached its climax in storage in a special depository, also had inevitable repercussions upon classification and cataloguing. For some time there was a growing fear that many classes of books were growing so large that the purposes of classification itself were being defeated: even with open access it was becoming impossible to see the forest for the trees. Restriction of material which goes onto the classified shelves helped somewhat. It reduced library expenditures for the technical processes of classifying, and even more for cataloguing.[13]

Next to the emergence of the dictionary catalogue, it was the production of gigantic printed catalogues which held the spotlight. We have already traced the history of the printed catalogues of the Bibliothèque Nationale and the British Museum. The latter, completed at the end of the last century, proved so valuable a bibliographical aid to libraries all over the world that the trustees decided to print a second, enlarged edition. Printing began in 1931, and volumes have continued to appear each year, though the war has slowed down their rate. Completion of the Bibliothèque Nationale catalogue was only prevented by the war. We have already mentioned the printing of *A Catalog of Books Represented by Library of Congress Printed Cards Issued to July 31, 1942.* Reproduced by photo-offset with a reduction in card size, this catalogue ran to 167 volumes and represented some 2,000,000 volumes in the Library of Congress for which cards were printed up to the terminal date. Supplements appeared regularly.[14]

The greatest project of its kind, however, was the printing of the German Union Catalogue *(Deutscher Gesamtkatalog).* At the end of the nineteenth century a union catalogue of Prussian libraries was begun on cards at the (then) Royal Library in Berlin. Shortly before the First World War plans were under way to begin printing, but the outbreak of hostilities put an end to them. The plans were revived in 1925 and after a vast amount of preliminary work the first volume appeared in 1931 as the *Union Catalogue of Prussian Libraries (Gesamtkatalog der preussischen Bibliotheken).* It listed the books printed before January 1, 1930 held by the Prussian State Library, the ten Prussian university libraries, the libraries of the four technical colleges, and the Academy of Braunsberg, and also the Bavarian State Library at Munich and the

National Library at Vienna. It was recognized from the beginning that the work ought to be expanded to include the holdings of more libraries. Beginning with the ninth volume (1936) the work became the *German Union Catalogue*. It then listed the holdings of about 100 libraries throughout greater Germany. The fourteen volumes published between 1931 and 1939 constitute a bibliographical tool of world-wide importance, and proved of great aid to the work of the German Loan Exchange (*Deutscher Leihverkehr*).[15] Books published after January 1, 1930 were listed in the *Berlin Accessions (Berliner Titeldrucke)* which thus becomes a supplement to making use of the *Gesamtkatalog*[16] as a printed catalogue of their collections by writing in their call numbers.

Provision of so thoroughgoing an inventory as the *German Union Catalogue* was one of the highlights of efforts made by scholars and librarians to take stock of their resources. No single library—and no group of libraries in any one nation—could fulfill all demands in this age of intensive scholarly research. A natural first recourse was the creation of union catalogues. Here Germany, as we have seen was formerly ahead of other nations. The Library of Congress, however, pushed its Union Catalog toward much greater inclusiveness. A large number of American libraries agreed to submit to the Union Catalog titles which they had and which were not to be found in the new Library of Congress printed catalogue. This provided a large proportion of titles unlisted in the Union Catalog, which was estimated to be about forty per cent of all titles held in American libraries. A movement which gained impetus and no lack of enthusiastic protagonists in the United States was the building up of regional—and even municipal—union catalogues. Many librarians looked askance, however, at the money and energy expended upon such projects and urged rather that the Union Catalog in Washington be enlarged.

Of equal value, perhaps, was the publication of a number of special bibliographies and inventories—many of them cooperative enterprises. Before the first World War, for example, there was the *International Catalogue of Scientific Literature*, published by the Royal Society. In 1927 a vast cooperative project of American and Canadian libraries culminated in publication of the *Union List of Serials*. So valuable did this prove that two supplements were called for, and in 1943 a greatly enlarged edition with careful bibliographical recension appeared, containing about 150,000 titles and listing the holdings of some 600 libraries. By 1945 publication of a supplement was necessary. Another great bibliographical enterprise is the *Union Catalogue of Incunabula (Gesamtkatalog der Wiegendrucke)*, the first volume of which was published in 1925 and which aimed to list all known incunabula.[17] We have already referred to the *Inventaire général des manuscrits des bibliothèques publiques de France*. Similar inventories in preparation in other countries were: for example, the *Verzeichnis der Handschriften im Deutschen Reich* and the *Catalogue général des manuscrits des bibliothèques de Belgique*. It would be a task in itself to enumerate the important specialized works in various fields that have appeared from 1900 to 1950.

The vast multiplication of research materials which led to union catalogues and special bibliographies brought to the fore the general problem of scholarly resources. This problem was seen most clearly in its national form: how to insure that all needed books shall be provided and that adequate collections shall be reasonably well distributed geographically. Such a problem was particularly acute for a large nation like the United States with its regional differences in culture and its heavy concentration of books in the northeast and southwest. In Germany a far-sighted move was taken during Althoff's regime in the Prussian Ministry of Education. The ten Prussian universities were assigned special fields in which to concentrate. As a result they built up special collections of high caliber while no one library had to undergo the strain of trying to cover all fields thoroughly. Efficient operation of the German Loan Exchange in conjunction with this acquisition policy went far toward meeting Germany's needs. In smaller countries, or in restricted regions, a number of cooperative arrangements were made. Thus in Denmark the Royal Library and the University Library in Copenhagen have an agreement whereby the former specializes in history, literature, and the humanities, and the latter in science, medicine and technology. There was a similar arrangement between the Swedish Royal Library and the Library of the Royal Academy of Sciences. In the United States several local agreements were made—for example, between Duke University and the University of North Carolina, and between libraries in metropolitan centers, such as New York and Chicago.

In the United States growing awareness of the problem led to surveys of library resources. Several studies were produced under the editorship of R.B. Downs, and the Special Libraries Association published a series of guides to selected special collections in the United States and Canada. Several years of war during which the main sources of foreign publications gradually went dry also served to make librarians and scholars acutely conscious of how important it was to have adequate coverage of this literature by American libraries. A program for cooperative acquisition of the important scholarly literature of the world was started in the United States. It called for voluntary assumption by libraries of carefully delimited fields in which they would take the responsibility of collecting exhaustively. In connection with comprehensive acquisition a classed catalogue also was proposed as a great inventory of scholarly materials.[18]

It will be recalled that during the last century there was a growing conviction of the importance of making librarianship a profession, culminating in moves to establish formal training for librarianship. Formal courses in librarianship were started at the University of Göttingen in 1886, being given by the eminent librarian Karl Dziatzko. A year later Melvil Dewey established the first library school in the United States.[19] Formal training for librarianship is over a century old, and it is possible to make some evaluation of it,[20] in terms of the time period under consideration.

As might be expected from their general library structure, Europe and America have differed in the kind of training devised for librarians. In Europe much emphasis was still put upon auxiliary sciences such as paleography, and in general upon the scholarly elements of the librarian's profession. In America more attention was paid to methods and technical processes, especially for public libraries. The École des Chartes in Paris probably represented the extreme of European training; indeed France did very little to provide training for assistants in popular libraries. Germany worked out a program compounded of theoretical instruction and practical apprenticeship. Althoff early recognized the necessity of setting standards, and the government organized examinations and grants certificates for two types of library work, the scholarly grade *(wissenschaftlicher Dienst)* for those who occupy the higher administrative posts in scholarly libraries, and the middle grade *(mittlerer Dienst)* for professional assistants in scholarly libraries and in popular libraries. Germany was most successful in attracting men of considerable scholarly ability into the profession, but attention to personnel for popular libraries increased largely through the efforts of men like Walter Hofmann, whose German School for Popular Libraries *(Deutsche Volksbüchereischule)* at Leipzig was the leading institution of its kind, and Wilhelm Krabbe at Berlin. The Third Reich supported training of personnel for popular libraries, recognizing their importance in influencing great masses of the people.

Many trained librarians in the Scandinavian countries went to the United States—or to Britain—for their training. In most of the other European countries formal library training was either so little organized or so recent that we shall pass them over. Russia, however, seemed to be developing long and intensive courses for her librarians, in which American and German methods were both adopted.

In Great Britain there was much reluctance for years to inaugurate formal courses. The Library Association tried to set certain minimum standards by giving examinations and granting certificates indicating various degrees of professional achievement. But British librarians themselves admitted that the system was not satisfactory. In 1919 the London University School for Librarianship was opened and courses were given in following years by several other universities, for example the National University of Wales. The British curriculum was a compromise between the German and American, with considerable emphasis upon auxiliary sciences. Until the school was closed in 1939 at the outbreak of war, the London School had not found acceptance in the profession such as was enjoyed by German or American schools.

In America library schools have grown fairly steadily in influence since their inception. There has been substantial agreement upon basic elements of the curriculum and general objectives, though not always upon adequacy of the achievement. The American Library Association encouraged a certain amount of uniformity, yet schools varied greatly in standards, in the quality of their instructors, and in the type of student. The critical Williamson report for the Carnegie Corporation[21] gave voice to dissatisfaction shared by many librarians. The Board of Education for Librarianship, and the Carnegie Corporation both put their weight behind certain recommendations of the report. Library schools were accredited according to definite professional criteria, and several new and excellent schools (among them California, Columbia [was reopened after the Williamson report], Michigan and Chicago) were founded. There is little doubt that a few good library schools had a salutary influence upon the profession. But there was also criticism—much of it justified—of the lack of scholarship among American librarians and the failure of library schools to improve the situation. The complaint came largely from reference libraries, which needed people with a scholarly background and administrative ability in key positions.

At this point, reference should be made to international cooperation and organizations in the field of library history in the period covered by this chapter. Cordial relations among individuals, groups, and nations have not been wanting. Panizzi's relations with German librarians of his generation have already been noted, and many European libraries have visited America with mutual profit. Close cooperation between Great Britain and the United States was a boon to the libraries of both countries. The reorganization of the Vatican Library with the advice and cooperation of the American commission had repercussions upon the entire library world. And no librarian could ever think of such beneficent organizations as the Carnegie and Rockefeller foundations without deep thankfulness.

The first international organization to achieve any influence was the International Federation of Documentation. This was founded in 1895 as the International Institute of Bibliography, and several times underwent changes of name and structural reorganization.[22] It undertook the ambitious project of compiling author and subject catalogues of the world's literature, but this was fulfilled only on a small scale. Much more successful was its work with the Dewey Decimal Classification. The so-called Brussels Expansion was published in several languages, and is used somewhat for library classification, and more widely for scientific, governmental (administrative), and commercial documentation. In microfilming the Federation was a real pioneer, foreseeing the importance of the new technique long before it became generally recognized. Microfilming enabled libraries to preserve materials threatened with deterioration, to conserve space by filming bulky materials such as newspapers, and to acquire textual reproductions of rare or valuable works. Its greatest value was been in documentation, as the experience of the National Archives in Washington already proved. The First World War dealt the Federation a staggering blow, from which it had not fully recovered when the second holocaust swept over Europe. But in the interim between wars the Federation patiently pursued its path and performed its function as a coordinating body by centralizing and distributing information about developments in scientific bibliography and documentation all over the world.

The League of Nations was responsible for the International Institute of Intellectual Cooperation. Its object is broad: to bring into contact intellectual workers of all kinds and in all countries. It stimulated exchange of information among national library bodies, sponsored meetings of librarians and bibliographers, and produced a number of valuable publications, among them the *Index Translationum* and studies of professional training[23] and popular libraries.[24]

In 1927, after several years of preliminary soundings, the International Federation of Library Associations was founded.[25] Despite subsequent world-wide economic depression the Federation kept functioning up to the outbreak of war, and resumed activity after the war. It had to its credit the working out of standard regulations for international library loans and the intangible but real benefits accruing from regular personal contacts between librarians of different nations. Valuable information on current library developments in various countries can be found in its publications.

One of the more significant trends of the post-World War One era was improvement of relations among the nations of the Western Hemisphere. The Library of Congress and the American Library associations were important agents in maintaining good relations. American librarians were invited to South America to give library instruction or to aid with such libraries as the Biblioteca Benjamin Franklin in Mexico City. Establishment of the Inter-American Library Assoiation, which held its first convention in 1938, gave evidence of the growth and seriousness of hemispheric cooperation.

The world wars, of course, had an adverse impact on libraries. In the U.S. during the First World War, for example, libraries were swept up in the anti-German hysteria and sentiment of the time, leading to the loss and destruction of a great deal of library materials. German-language sources, as well as materials dealing not only with German history, literature, and culture, but German-Americana as well were often discarded, destroyed, or sent to storage. For further information on this period, see Wayne Wiegand, *An Active Instrument for Propaganda: The American Public Library During*

World War I. (Westport, Conn.: Greenwood Press, 1989). Also, see Don Heinrich Tolzmann, ed., *German-Americans and the World Wars.* (München: K.G. Saur, 1995-98). The rise of fascism and Nazism and the outbreak of the Second World War, of course, had immediate impact on European libraries, and found expression not only in censorship, governmental control, but in the removal and destruction of library materials, especially of works by authors considered undesirable by totalitarian regimes. Even more catastrophic destruction occurred as a result of the war. The war itself with bombing raids of civilian centers brought with it the partial and complete destruction of libraries. For example, the war is estimated to have led to the destruction of one-third of the public libraries in Germany alone.

After the war, the Soviet Union absconded with the holdings of numerous libraries and archives, which it considered as war booty. A documentary study of the library holdings removed from Germany by the Soviet Union after the Second World War is found in Klaus-Dieter Lehmann and Ingo Kolasa, *Die Trophäenkommissionen der Roten Armee: Eine Dokumentensammlung zur Verschleppung von Büchern aus deutschen Bibliotheken* (Frankfurt am Main: Vittorio Klostermann, 1996).

To Make a Bonfire of German Books.

CLEVELAND, April 4. — A German propaganda bonfire–the flames fed by German schoolbooks,–literature,war screeds, music, phonograph records, and pictures–is being planned in this city for either Saturday or Monday night. Huge boxes for the collection of material for the bonfire will be placed in downtown sections by those in charge of the movement.

New York Times
5 April, 1918, 24:2

HUGE BONFIRE PLANNED

BY HIGH SCHOOL PUPILS TO DESTROY GERMAN TEXT BOOKS

SPECIAL DISPATCH TO THE ENQUIRER

Cleveland, Ohio, April 2. — The German language will not be taught in the Chagrin Falls High School after this week. This was the ultimatum issued today by students of that institution, following action of the Board of Education yesterday to abolish the language at the end of the school year.

Despite action of the board, the students were insistent that the language will not be taught after this week.

Rumors were current to-day that the students are planning to enter the school building at night, remove their textbooks and burn them in a huge bonfire to be started in the village square Saturday night on the occasion of the celebration of Liberty Day. Many students said they would throw all German books on the fire.

The Department of Justice is conducting an investigation into the situation. Six government agents attended the board meeting last night.

Enquirer, Cincinnati
4 April, 1918, p. 9

Figure 43: How much was destroyed during the World Wars?

Chapter XI. Into The Information Age

The later half of the twentieth century has witnessed numerous dramatic changes with the advent of the so-called information, or electronic age. The purpose of this chapter is to provide a global survey of developments in the world of libraries since the period of the middle of the 20th century to the present. As such, it makes no attempt at a detailed historical account of developments in any particular area or country, but rather aims at providing a general sense of what the trends have been in the past half century, together with some comments regarding future developments.[1]

The unprecedented growth and development of the U.S. projected America to the very forefront of library development in the latter half of the twentieth century, whereas in Europe the widespread devastation caused by two world wars in the first half of the century contributed to the libraries there taking a secondary position in the world, while those elsewhere, such as Africa, Latin America, and Asia, had to await the end of the colonial era and the establishment of nationhood before the question of library service could be addressed..

By 1960, the Federal Republic of Germany had basically rebuilt its library system as a result of widespread destruction during the war and the subsequent division of the country. The fall of the Berlin Wall and the reunification of Germany in 1990 led to the question of reunifying the library system of the Federal Republic with those of the German Democratic Republic. This led to the merging of the national libraries in Frankfurt and Leipzig into a new institution under the old name, *Deutsche Nationalbibliothek*. The library in Leipzig aimed to concentrate on bibliographic services to the German book trade, the preservation and conservation processes, and a planned museum for books and writing, while the library in Frankfurt am Main planned to compile and publish the German national bibliography, sponsor information and communication activities, which would include hosting IFLA Universal Bibliographic Control-Informational MARC (UBC-IM) program.

Hence, the two national bibliographies from Leipzig and Frankfurt am Main were combined under the direction of the latter library, but it retained its former title, *Deutsche Nationalbibliographie*, from January 1991 onwards. The libraries in Berlin, the *Deutsche Staatsbibliothek* (east) and the *Staatsbibliothek Preussicher Kulturbesitz* (west) were merged as the *Deutsche Staatsbibliothek* as a single institution with two locations. The eastern library was assigned the task of collecting pre-1945 materials, while the western library took on that of post-1945 materials, thus resolving the split between the old and rare materials that had been relocated in the west during the war for security purposes and their catalogue descriptions which had remained in the east.

The *Zentralinstitut für Bibliothekswesen* and the *Methodisches Zentrum* were merged with the *Deutsches Bibliotheksinstitut* in Berlin, and the two major professional journals, the *Zentralblatt für Bibliothekswesen* and the *Zeitschrift für Bibliothekswesen*, merged under the latter name. Also, the publications of the book trade associations merged together as the *Boersenblatt für den deutschen Buchhandel*.

An examination of the libraries in the east revealed a number of substantial deficiencies and weaknesses in terms of collections and facilities. However, it appears that public libraries contained a great deal of what may have been considered subversive or anti-government literature. Most libraries lacked basic supplies and equipment, such as photocopy machines. Funds were promised, however, to address these deficiencies. Also, it should be noted that donations from institutions and individuals have been sought to build library collections, not only from the Federal Republic, but also, from the U.S. After unification, discussions in the profession focused on how to standardize library education in Germany and to bring it into harmony with library education in the European Community. No doubt, it will take a number of years before these various efforts will bear fruit in terms of collections and facilities, as well as in the area of library education.

France was also, of course, affected by the two world wars, but the early conquest of the country in the Second World War resulted in the absence of the kinds of losses of library resources suffered elsewhere. A new era began for the Bibliothéque Nationale in 1988 when François Mitterand, President of the French Republic, made the announcement regarding plans to build "one of the largest and most modern libraries in the world." Perrault then designed a huge structure for a site located at Tolbiac in the eastern part of Paris. This would provide place for 4,200 seats and stacks for 15 million books. To prepare for the move (1999) the BN began a number of programs, including a complete inventory of its collections, an automated circulation system, a national union catalog, a preservation program, a new integrated computer system, and a Technical Center for the Book. For the union catalog, a retroconversion program was begun, which included a few university and public library collections as well.

Libraries in France are highly centralized. In 1945, a Direction de Bibliotheques was created in the Ministry of Education, and this controlled the BN, university libraries, department lending libraries, and some major municipal libraries. This system was divided in 1975, 1981, and 1986, so that university libraries remained with the Ministry of Education and the BN and public libraries came under the Ministry of Culture. The departments took on responsibility for provincial lending libraries and communes that of the municipal libraries.

General Inspectors are appointed who visit libraries of all categories, university and public, to ascertain the quality and efficiency of libraries, as well as to advise on related matters, and to assess requests for grants, and provide other library-related services. In 1989, the National Council for Libraries was established, which advises government on library issues for the purpose of creating an efficient library network, including such matters as the national union catalog.

The library profession in France consists of civil servants and documentalists, with the former being recruited by national competitive examinations and work in libraries managed by the government, whereas the latter are trained at the INTD, the *Institut Nationale des Techniques de la Documentation,* or at one of the few private schools. There are several professional library associations which reflect this division of the professions in France. Library education also reflects the various categories of librarianship: 1. civil servants in most of the state-supported institutions; 2. civil servants in local and regional institutions; and, 3. documentalists working in private or semi-private documentation centers. Each category, it should be noted, has its own training programs.

Recent efforts in Italy witnessed improvements in the national library system by means of the launching of the SBN (National Library Service), which was an important step in the direction of creating a national union catalog and a national lending system. By 1990, more than 200 libraries had joined in this program, which reflected holdings consisting of 35 million volumes. Altogether, ten institutions function as national libraries in Italy, the most prominent of which are the National Central Libraries in Rome and Florence. The Library of Rome, officially known as the Biblioteca Naziolnale Centrale Vittorio Emanuele II, collaborates with its sister Central Library in Florence, to produce bibliographies of Italian and foreign materials.

The library in Rome specializes in lending, whereas Florence serves a major national archive. The library in Rome contains about 4.5 million volumes in its collections. Other national libraries are found in: Bari, Milan, Naples, Paltermo, Turin, Venice, Potenza, and Dosenza.

It is said that Italian libraries are characterized by administrative chaos, and that this is due to the fact that a unified Italy appeared late on the scene in the 1860s. This is seen in the area of academic libraries, as there are twelve university libraries, each of which is under the administration of its respective university, but, like the national libraries, all of which are dependent on the state for funding. One of the major areas of progress was with regard to the project SBN, which aimed to link university libraries not only together, but also with foreign libraries with similar collections. Also, in 1989 the government placed university administration under the Ministry of University and Scientific Research, as it previously had under the Ministry of Public Instruction. The placement of libraries with research has steadily improved the status of academic libraries in terms of the support they receive, as well as their stature.

Not until the 1970s was there a real network of public libraries in Italy. Some had existed due to private local, or philanthropic support. The Fascist government had broken up the federation of public libraries founded in 1908, and after the Second World War, public libraries were neglected. In 1972 and 1977, the government turned control of these libraries over to the local regions in which they were located, and not all of them supported them adequately, thus resulting in a rather uneven system of public libraries in Italy.

Italian librarians are under national, regional, provincial, and local administrations, all of which have a variety of views regarding the support of libraries, which means that some libraries have professional librarians, while others do not. Degrees in library science are only fairly recent in Italian higher education, and a prerequisite is that one must first earn a general university degree. The Italian Library Association publishes AIB Notizie, a monthly newsletter, as well as a quarterly, the Bollettino d'Informazioni. Among its major concerns, is the effort to focus on the recognition of librarianship as a profession and the promotion of legislation to restructure the national library system.

Britain's libraries suffered losses as a result of the Second World War, especially during the bombing of London, although the libraries of Oxford and Cambridge survived relatively well. However, postwar library development was impaired somewhat by the fact that library funding depended on local, rather than national funding, as was the case in France, where libraries are, as noted, highly centralized. A major development occurred in 1972 with the passage of the British Library Act, which was a public statement of faith in Library of the British Museum. This led to the creation of the British Library in 1973, as a merger of the British Museum Library, The National Library for Science and Technology., the Patent Office Library, the Science Reference Library, and the staff of the British National Bibliography. The BL, hence, became the storehouse of the written record, but also a repository of information serving the full gamut of informational needs.

After two decades, it was realized that the BL needed new quarters. By bringing together this wealth of library materials at one site, the BL further enhanced its stature as a library of major importance. Estimates at to the total collection size of the BL exceed 100,000,000. The latest information regarding the BL can be found in The British Library Journal. The new building at St. Pancras, which opened in 1998, was designed to consolidate all of the various collections scattered across London. The first phase of plans, scheduled for completion in 1993, provided for an area of 80,000 sq.m., with 579 readers seats, 12.7 kilometers of open-access shelving, and 292 km of closed-access shelving. The second phase, which was scheduled for 1997, provided for an additional 35,000 sq. m., with an additional 627 reader seats, 10.5 km of open-access shelving, and 23 km closed-access shelving. The architects were Colin St. John Wilson and Partners.

Other national libraries in Britain are the National Library of Scotland and the National Library of Wales. The former dates to 1682, and is housed in a building on George IV Bridge, Edinburgh, and acquires 100,000 volumes annually, and specializes in Scottish books and manuscripts. The National Library of Wales dates to 1911, and maintains a collection of more than two million printed books, and specializes in Welsh materials.

Britain has many fine academic libraries, such as those at the older universities of Oxford and Cambridge. Indeed, England's oldest surviving college library building is at Oxford University's Merton College, founded in 1264. As noted, public libraries were hampered by their dependence on local authorities. The London Governmental Act of 1963, the Public Libraries Museum Act of 1964, and Local Government Act of 1973, with separate legislation for Scotland and Northern Ireland, reduced the number of local library authorities to 167. The result of the creation of larger authorities responsible for libraries resulted in units more financially viable to support library services at the local level. In spite of budget cuts in industrial areas in the 1980s, public library systems have, hence, continued to grow and develop.

It should be noted that British public libraries are among the most heavily used in the world, as by the mid-1990s, there were 568,000 loans, or just more than 10 per capita. Also, it should be noted that the larger public libraries in urban areas often tend to have more in common with a research library than do smaller public libraries. For example, the Shakespeare collection of the Birmingham City Library can be mentioned in this regard. This is true also in the U.S.; for example, the Boston Public Library.

The Library Association, founded in 1877, continues to serve the profession in Britain, and Aslib serves the needs of special libraries and information bureaus. By the mid-1990s, there were 16 library schools in Britain, the oldest being the University College in London, founded in 1919. The other schools came into being after the Second World War. All are attached to universities.

In 1985, Britain established the Transbinary Study Group on Librarianship and Information Studies, which was charged with examining library education in the United Kingdom. This has led to efforts to bring the profession into the Information Age. As a result, Leeds, began offering a B.A. in Librarianship, as well as a B.Sc. in Information Science. Sheffield changed its name of its school to the Department of Information Studies, and Strathclyde became a Department of Information Science, which is part of the Business School. It might also be noted with regard to library education in Britain that the Library Association in 1986 voted to recognize courses taken at programs accredited by the American and Australian Library Associations as equivalent to those taken at programs approved by the Library Association in so far as gaining admission to a British library school is concerned.

In the totalitarian state of the Soviet Union, library service fulfilled the standard functions of the library, but also rendered ideological service to the state. Before the war, a substantial public library system under the aegis of state control had been established, and after the war great sums were expended on behalf of libraries in the Soviet Union. The fall of Communism resulted in the end of this strictly controlled state library system, as well as the loss of funding from the state, resulting in the closing of numerous libraries, some of which were left abandoned.

It should be noted that the U.S.S.R. consisted of fifteen Union Republics, including the largest, the Russian Soviet Federated Republic, so that where there was previously one library system to speak of, there are now fifteen. In Russia, the former national libraries, the Russian State Library, previously the Lenin Library, and the Russian National Library, previously the Salykov-Schedrin State Public library, were renamed, and opened to the general public for the first time. The holdings of the Russian State Library were found to be forty percent larger than had been anticipated. Thus far, the fiscal problems in the new Russian economy have, of course, adversely influenced the Russian library system, and it and it most likely will take into the next century for libraries in Russia before it can be ascertained what the results of the 1990s funding shortfalls will have been. In like measure, Russian academic libraries suffer from fiscal problems, so that it will take in to the next century before the situation with them is also stabilized. Russian public libraries number more than 60,000, and are the responsibility of the Russian Ministry of Culture. After the fall of the Soviet Union, censorship in the area of public libraries was eliminated, and they were opened as they never had been before. As with other libraries, public libraries were also hard hit by the economic problems facing the new Russia. In 1991, the responsibility for these public libraries was divided up among federal, regional, and local authorities. Some of these are now in a most difficult situation, and suffer from a drastic loss of funding, so that it will take years for the public library system in Russia to be placed on a sound fiscal foundation.

Although information on the status of libraries in the other former Soviet republic is difficult to obtain, some of the developments on the libraries of the new independent, democratic republic, Ukraine, are available. The V.I. Vernadsky Central Scientific Library, which is the research library of the Ukrainian Academy of Sciences, is without question the largest library in Ukraine, and functions as the national library. Its collections house ca. 12,500,00 volumes. Among its collections, is a valuable collection of rare materials is the Assyrian-Babylonian book list from the third century B.C. Plans in the future call for the development of a union catalog of library holdings in Ukraine. In terms of academic libraries reference should be made to the Taras Shevchenko Kiev State University, established in 1834, which now has a library with a Scientific-Technical Library of Ukraine, founded in 1935, houses more than twenty million volumes dealing with science and technology, and coordinates the work of scientific libraries in Ukraine. In terms of public libraries, the Ministry of Culture bears responsibility for 22,000 of them, the most important of which is undoubtedly the State Library of the Ukraine in Kiev, which was founded in 1866, and contains more than four million volumes. After independence in 1991, library educators began reforms to model library education after that in the U.S.

In the U.S., libraries experienced a tremendous growth surge in the last half of the twentieth century. In the 1940s, it was estimated that libraries were doubling in size approximately every fifteen years. This constant growth and development caused those in the library world to be ever involved with the re-designing of existing library structures, with the re-organization of services, and with the allocation of ever-increasing funds for library systems. This latter problem was partially addressed with federal funding for college and university libraries in the 1950s and 1960s. There were federal programs established for the acquisition of library materials, the construction of buildings, and the education and employment of professional librarians. All of these factors contributed to U.S. libraries taking on a major leadership role in the world with regard to library developments in the academic area.

Library education underwent sweeping changes after the completion of the *Williamson Report* in 1919, a report by C.C. Williamson, which had been funded by the Carnegie Corporation of New York. Recommendations included the need to locate library education at universities so that it could be established as an academic field and so that it would be developed within a professional framework. This new emphasis allowed for librarianship to grow and develop as a profession based on academic foundations. Also, the need was emphasized that such library programs were in need of accreditation. These proposals were by and large accepted and became the foundation for the emergence of the profession of librarianship based on library science as an academic field.

These developments were further enhanced in 1928 with the establishment of the Graduate Library School at the University of Chicago, which paved the way for graduate research and study at the doctoral level. It was City College of New York which funded the establishment of the Chicago School, it should be noted. Graduate programs now emerged offering doctoral degrees, which led to the strengthening of library programs across the country, which now were staffed by faculty with these degrees.

The great funding afforded education in the postwar era led to the continued growth and development of library educational programs, so that by the mid-1980s there were a total of 56 accredited programs. Economic recession caused a number of programs to either be cut back, or eliminated at that time, including those at Columbia and Chicago. Others began to re-assess their programs and curricula in the light of the impact of the information age. Indeed, this kind of program review may be viewed as similar to the re-structuring of the field in the 1920s. By the late 1990s there was a total of 49 accredited programs

Core curricula were revamped, and library schools even renamed themselves, now often becoming schools of library and information science. Some programs entered into cooperative ventures with other programs, such as computer science, communications, electronic media, etc. All of these developments further reflect the growth and development and on-going evolution of the field of library science. They indicate the increased diversification of the field, as it addresses the universe of library and information needs of the day.

By mid century most American municipalities had established local funding for public libraries, and states had provided state funding for libraries in rural areas. Public libraries also benefited from federal funding in the 1960s as a result of the programs of the Great Society under Lyndon Johnson, which provided funds for construction, the acquisition of library materials, and the creation of outreach programs. Another development in the U.S., was the establishment of library service by means of the creation of school libraries, which received substantial federal funding in the 1950s and 1960s. This period witnessed the establishment of literally thousands of school libraries across the country, thereby bringing library materials into areas, where there might not have been any other kind of library available.

Several acts of the federal government, beginning with the Library Services Act of 1965 greatly influenced the development of libraries at the state level. These acts provided for federal funding through the state library, and were applied to a wide variety of programs to assist libraries, including surveys, equipment and supplies, bookmobiles, as well as, of course, for books and materials for public libraries. Often, these funds were matched by funds provided by the states, so that by 1962 the states were spending three times what the federal government was for libraries. In the 1980s, due to federal budgetary cutbacks, these kinds of programs experienced a loss of funding, and had to be restructured given the funding realities, but there is no question that for roughly three decades, from the mid-1960s into the 1980s, that the LSA and other acts greatly impacted on public libraries across the country, as well as all types of libraries.

A number of private research libraries were established in the twentieth century, which grew to fruition during this period, including the Huntington Library in San Marino, California; the Folger Shakespeare Library in Washington, D.C.; the Newberry Library and Crerar Libraries in Chicago. The latter is now part of the library system of the University of Chicago. In the various states, the archives established to function as the state archives for state governments and legislatures were further developed, as were state historical societies. A particularly sharp increase was noted in the establishment of special libraries by business and industry to serve the particular needs of a group of users. Many of these were at the forefront of technological advances in the library field in the latter part of the century, especially in the area of information storage and retrieval.

Of major importance in the U.S. was the Library of Congress, which served a threefold purpose of service as the library for members of Congress, as the major scholarly library in the U.S., and as the leadership institution in the library field. Indeed, the Library of Congress functioned not only as a national leader, but internationally can be viewed as perhaps the major scholarly library in the world, with a collection in the 1990s encompassing more than twenty million volumes, a staff of five thousand, and a budget in excess of three hundred million. Many of its collections are of international significance. For example, the largest German collection in the world is found in the Library of Congress.[2]

Herbert Putnam, who became Librarian of Congress in 1899, strongly promoted the Library of Congress as the national library, efforts which continued in the latter half of the century. Early in the century, L.C. began distribution of catalog cards, and this grew into the National Union Catalogue and ultimately into MARC (Machine Readable Cataloging) tapes. It also continued on its national leadership efforts, actively investigating preservation programs,. Sponsoring book exchanges, and became the center for the National Library Services for the Blind and Physically Handicapped. It also established the Center for the Book to emphasize the importance of books in history.

In 1984, Congress approved an appropriation of $81.5 million for the restoration of the Jefferson and Adams buildings of the Library of Congress, and work began in 1986, with Phase I completed in 1989, and Phase II completed in 1994. In 1995, congress approved an additional $2.5 million for the renovation of the Coolidge Auditorium and the Whittall Pavilion, and this work was completed in 1996. In 1997, the Jefferson Building was reopened on the occasion of its 100th anniversary, with a ribbon-cutting ceremony and a public "Festival of Cultures."

An exhibit brochure entitled American Treasures of the Library of Congress highlights the holdings of L. C., especially in a section on "Building the National Collection," which describes the library as follows:

In 1800, Congress set aside $5,000 "for the purchase of such books as may be necessary for the use of Congress . . . and for fitting up a suitable apartment for containing them and for placing them therein." In 1815, Congress spent nearly $24,000 to buy Thomas Jefferson's library, comprising nearly twice as many books as those burned by the British near the end of the War of 1812. The appropriation of such large sums for books indicates that from the beginning, American statesmen have viewed a library not as a luxury, but as an essential working tool for the creation and maintenance of a healthy democracy.

The Library continues to receive money annually from Congress to purchase books and other library materials, but that amount is a small fraction of the value of the Library's annual acquisitions. What had been a slow but steady growth of the collections in the nineteenth century exploded in 1870, the year that the Copyright Office was transferred into the Library of Congress. From then on, all creators wishing to protect their intellectual property rights by registering their created work with the office were required to deposit a copy of that work in the Library. It is the cumulative record of copyright deposits that has so profoundly shaped the collections and transformed the congressional library into the memory bank of the nation. For it is not only writers who register for copyright, but composers, engravers, cartoonists, map makers, musical arrangers, photographers, film makers, recording artists, poster designers, architects, engineers, speech writers, journalists, scriptwriters, advertising artists, comic book publishers, software writers, and many others. Their deposits have added to the

Library's record of American creativity. Donation is another invaluable source of the collections, especially in the area of personal papers and rare items. A third source of materials is transfer from government agencies. Many maps have come this way, as well as works created for special government programs, such as the Federal Theatre Project Archives and the Farm Security Administration photographs from the 1930s and 1940s.

If Jefferson were alive today, his collection would no doubt include all the new media that have appeared since his time—sound recordings, films, photographs, and CD-ROMS. His conviction that the congressional library should be universal in scope continues to inform the daily decisions about what the Library acquires. For it is here that the nation's great experiment in democracy is recorded, and here that this generation and future generations can learn for themselves who they are and where they came from.

In 1976, the American Library Association celebrated its centennial with a variety of events and activities, the ALA continued to enjoy growth and development in the following years with membership surpassing 55,000, and its revenues doubling to more than $24 million. Although organized for the American library profession, the ALA clearly has world-wide influence, and is looked to for leadership by libraries and library associations everywhere. Among the agendas, which it continues to address are the following: the maintenance of professional standards for the field of librarianship; the right to access to information; the improvement of opportunities for women and minorities; the defense of intellectual freedom; the improvement of funding for libraries; the emergence of information science; and the evolution of the field of library science, including the need to continually revitalize professional education in terms of present developments and demands.

In areas outside of Europe and the U.S., library systems could be viewed as only entering their beginning stages of development. In various countries, library developments were much less systematic and organized, and lacked the necessary funding. For example, in Asia, library development had to await the end of the period of colonial rule before addressing the question of the status of libraries. An exception, of course, was in China, where as in the Soviet Union, a great deal of emphasis was placed on libraries, particularly on the establishment of the National Library of China, considered one of the major libraries in the world. Also, exceptional libraries could also be found in Japan, whose libraries are the most advanced in Asia. For further information on libraries in China and Japan, See Priscilla C. Yu, *Chinese Academic and Research Libraries: Acquisitions, Collections, and Organizations.* (Greenwich, Conn.: JAI Pr., 1997) and Theodore F. Welch, *Libraries and Librarianship in Japan.* (Westport, Conn.: Greenwood Pr., 1997).

In Africa, the picture was bleaker than in Asia, as the continent was engulfed with warfare, revolution, famine, and other internal socio-economic and political problems, so that questions of library affairs were not even on the agenda. Once established as independent nations, some progress was made, as in the case of Ethiopia, founded by Haile Selassie in 1944, and which then established a national library. By 1961, the University of Addis Ababa had been established, and a library founded there. However, as is indicative elsewhere, the libraries here had to struggle with the lack of funding, the indifference of government, and political instability. Further improvements in Africa will require greater political stability and increased funding well into the next century. For further information on the status of libraries in Africa, see R.P. Sturges, *The Quiet Struggle: Libraries and Information for Africa.* (London: Mansell, 1990).

Libraries in Latin America, by the latter half of the century, had formed a rather well developed system of public, school, and academic libraries, so that today there are in Latin America twenty-five university libraries and more than fifteen hundred public libraries. In the smaller countries, library development is behind those of the larger nations, but is nonetheless slowly expanding. Regarding libraries in Latin America, see the latest edition of *World Guide to Libraries.* (München: K.G. Saur), which provides a comprehensive guide to libraries around the world. It is organized in terms of the following categories: national libraries; general research libraries; university libraries, college libraries; professional school libraries, school libraries; government libraries; ecclesiastical libraries; corporate, business libraries; special libraries maintained by other institutions; and public libraries. This world directory of libraries is useful in providing a statistical picture on a global basis of just how many libraries there are. It lists libraries with holdings of more than 30,000 volumes and special libraries with more than 5,000 volumes. Altogether, there were, by the mid-1990s, 45,773 such libraries in 181 countries around the world.

This survey of world-wide library affairs provides the general context for a consideration of what may be called the advent of the information, or electronic age, which brought dramatic and profound change in the world of libraries. Indeed, some no longer spoke of libraries, but rather of information centers in reflection of entering this new historical period. The electronic information age was marked by the emergence to central importance of the computer in the library world, new telecommunication networks, and new kinds of information systems, such as the World Wide Web. By the close of the century, almost every aspect of life is touched in some way by computers, including banking, business, industry, education, etc.

Some advocated the creation of a "paperless" society and foresaw the end of the era of books and libraries and the creation of virtual libraries, which could embrace all that could be found in the world's libraries and archives, thus causing some in the latter to have more than their share of misgivings about such prophecies. Most, however, viewed the information age practically in terms of the benefits provided in the accessing of information on a heretofore unimaginable scale, and the new age was becoming one, which would not replace libraries and books, but rather greatly enhance and facilitate accessing them.

However, some dissension was bound to arise, as was, for example, the case in 1991 when plans ensued for the construction of a new building to house the Bibliotheque de France. Critical opposition arose with regard to the architects who claimed that in the future there would be no books, but rather a paperless virtual library. Another project, which aroused discussion was the American Memory Project of the Library of Congress, which aims to transfer the Library's holdings to machine-readable form. In some there arose questions as to whether there was an attempt to replace, rather than supplement already existing library systems. Such debates are perhaps to be expected given the nature of the dramatic developments.

Among the practical innovations of the computerization of libraries has been the introduction of online public access catalogs to access library holdings, a trend becoming relatively wide spread in the U.S., Germany, and Japan especially by the end of the twentieth century. This will also become increasingly the case with other countries and areas around the world in the twenty-first century. This will also become increasingly the case with other countries and areas around the world in the twenty-first century. This has increasingly linked collections, libraries, and archives around the globe. This has, of course, resulted in the replacement of card catalogs with online systems. Such catalogs also provide access to an array of databases, indexes, abstracts, the World Wide Web, and other kinds of information systems. Rather than negotiating a card catalog, library users now make use of individual work-stations providing access to a worldwide array of sources.

Major online bibliographic networks have also been established, such as OCLC, the Online Computer Library Center in Columbus, Ohio, which was designed to assist libraries in the cataloging of library materials by providing online access to the libraries of several thousand libraries. This also serves as a union catalog, which enables the user to identify a publication and its library location. Other countries have tried as well to establish similar systems.[3]

As information and how to access it becomes an increasingly important item, it has also become increasingly of value. This has resulted in the information industry, which provides information, as well as informational produces and services on a fee basis, thus also influencing libraries to introduce fee-based services.

In the twenty-first century libraries will continue to evolve in concert with the information/electronic age. This will mean increasing accessibility by means of computerized access to collections world-wide and library materials will become increasingly available online, beginning with journals, newspapers and other serial publications. Also, images and texts of various kinds of publications, including rare and unique books, will also become ever more accessible and available online, thus protecting them and contributing to their preservation. Regardless of the informational format, however, libraries will continue to collect, preserve, organize and make informational sources available, and such materials will include the entire universe of formats ranging from print to non-print materials, including materials ranging from clay tablets, papyrus scrolls, books, through electronic informational sources.[4]

UCLID   UC's Online Catalog

University of Cincinnati Libraries

Welcome to the University of Cincinnati Libraries Catalog

You may search for library materials using the following:

- AUTHOR
- TITLE
- KEYWORD
- SUBJECT
- MEDICAL SUBJECT
- UNIFORM TITLE/SERIES
- CALL NUMBER & NUMERIC INDEXES

Change Your Search by Location or Material Type   Featured Resources

- OhioLINK CENTRAL CATALOG
- Library INFORMATION
- **RESERVES:**COURSE NAME or INSTRUCTOR

- VIEW YOUR OWN LIBRARY RECORD

- MATERIALS I would like the library to acquire

| Welcome | Catalog Menu | Information

OHIOLINK CENTRAL CATALOG

OhioLINK Central Catalog

Ohio Library and Information Network

You may search Statewide for library materials using the following:

TITLE	AUTHOR
SUBJECT	MEDICAL SUBJECT
WORDS In Title, Author, Subject, Notes, Publisher	
Call Number	Other Numbers

Library of Congress	Dewey Decimal	NLM SuDoc	ISBN ISSN	OCLC	Other

Search Tips and Information About This Catalog

Figure 44, Figure 45: Website for the OhioLINK Central Catalog.

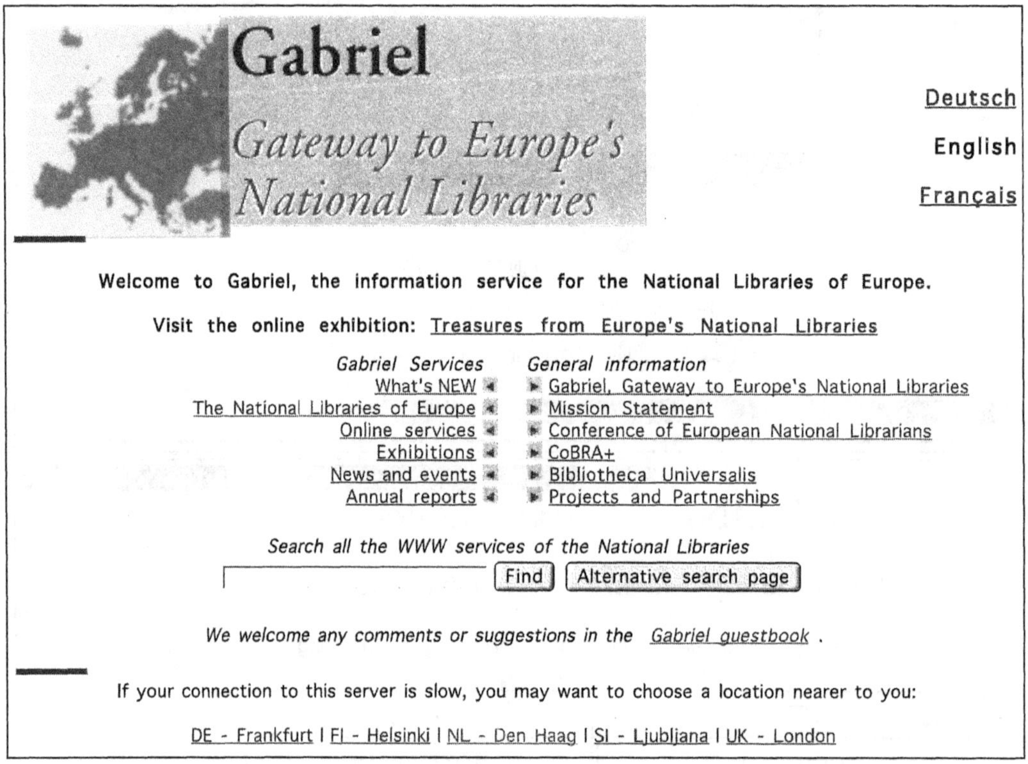

Figure 46: Website for Gabriel, the gateway to Europe's national libraries.

Online Catalog (Library of Congress)

LIBRARY OF CONGRESS ONLINE CATALOG

The Library of Congress Online Catalog (http://catalog.loc.gov/) is a database of approximately 12 million records representing books, serials, computer files, manuscripts, cartographic materials, music, sound recordings, and visual materials in the Library's collections. The Online Catalog also provides references, notes, circulation status, and information about materials still in the acquisitions stage. Text-only users, please see special information on an alternative interface for the online catalog.

Search the Online Catalog

Hours: 24 hours a day, seven days a week *
* Maintenance and updates are done during the late evening
and early morning hours, during which time some features may not be available.

Alternative Interface for the Online Catalog

Although, the primary interface to the Online Catalog is available at http://catalog.loc.gov/, this interface does not work well for text-based Web browsers (e.g., *Lynx*). In addition, for security reasons, the Library is not able to offer any Telnet access to the Online Catalog. An alternative interface is currently available that does work well for text-based browsers using the Library's Z39.50 Gateway (learn more about the Z39.50 protocol for information retrieval).

The alternative interface **does not** provide the following information and features found in the primary Web interface:

- availability and location(s) in the Library for materials
- circulation status of any item
- number of copies available
- ability to limit searches by date, language, material type, country of publication, etc.

Simple Search	Advanced Search	Phrase Search
any keyword	multiple terms using Boolean operators	left-anchored, exact phrase

Hours: 24 hours a day, seven days a week *
* Maintenance and updates are done during the late evening
and early morning hours, during which time some features may not be available.
This service is currently limited to 250 simultaneous users.

Library of Congress Home | Using the Library | Thomas | Copyright Office | American Memory | Exhibitions | The Library Today | Bicentennial | Help & FAQs | Search our Site | Site Map

Library of Congress
Comments: lcweb@loc.gov (September 26, 2000)

Figure 47: Website for the Library of Congress.

LibDex - The Library Index

LIBDEX
THE LIBRARY INDEX

Search across millions of documents within Electric Library!

ELECTRIC LIBRARY
[ ] Go!

Browse 16,633 libraries

What is Libdex? ::: Country ::: OPAC Vendor

Fundraising ::: Friends of Libraries ::: What's New

Open Directory ::: Library News Daily ::: Publishers

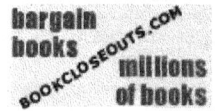

Search for Libraries

[ ] go

Enter **one** keyword or phrase from library name.

Our Sponsors

bargain books
BOOKCLOSEOUTS.COM
millions of books

Your comments on Libdex?

Copyright © 2000, Northern Lights Internet Solutions Ltd. Privacy Policy
E-Mail Peter Scott

HOME | ADD YOUR LIBRARY | UPDATE YOUR LIBRARY | RECOMMEND THIS SITE

Figure 48: Website for LIBDEX, which provides access to thousands of libraries.

Although the world has fully entered the electronic age by the threshold of the 21st century, its full impact has not, of course, been realized. Indeed, only some of its initial stages have been reached. It should be noted that electronic computers were only invented in the 1940s and word processors in the 1980s. Thus, the information age has only just begun, but its impact in the 21st century is bound to be as deep and thoroughgoing as was the revolution begun in the 15th century by the invention of printing.

In gauging the full impact of the information age, perhaps some hints as to how extensive this will be can be ascertained by way of comparison to the earlier printing revolution, as we now move from the print age to the electronic age. In describing the printing revolution S.H. Steinberg observed in his *Five Hundred Years of Printing*:

> "The history of printing is an integral part of the general history of civilization. The principal vehicle for the conveyance of ideas during the past five centuries, printing touches upon, and often penetrates, almost every sphere of human activity. Neither political, constitutional, ecclesiastical, and economic events, nor sociological, philosophical, and literary movements can be fully understood without taking into account the influence which the printing press has exerted upon them."[5]

The new information age will unquestionably be as influential and revolutionary in terms of its impact, as have been the preceding five centuries as a result of the invention of printing. How does this all impact on libraries? Again by way of comparison, we can see the invention of printing had a dramatic impact on libraries, which became institutions for the diffusion of knowledge and information, and became ever more accessible. The information age likewise promises the increasing accessibility of information on a global scale with libraries, or information centers, playing a key role in this diffusion of knowledge and information, as they have in the past.

To return to the maxim—libraries are the memory of mankind—it should be noted that the purpose of this work has been to trace the history of libraries. History itself is simply the record of the past, not the future. Hence, it is obviously beyond the scope of this work to predict the future developments in the realm of library history. However, some of the predictions made about how things would stand in the library world by the latter 20th century can be evaluated now that this time period has been attained.

It was in the 1960s, that the notion emerged that by the end of the century a paperless society would be at hand. In 1962, Marshall McLuhan published his highly influential *The Gutenberg Galaxy*, which claimed that media would lead to the elimination of the print era.[6] In 1980, F. Wilfrid Lancaster maintained in his *The*

Impact of a Paperless Society on Research Library of the Future, that there would be a decline of artifacts, such as the book, as the primary vehicle for information storage and retrieval, and that these would be replaced by electronically accessible forms of data, so that in essence a paperless society was emerging.[7] In 1982, James Thompson wrote in *The End of Libraries*, that computers would eventually displace the part of "mankind's book-centered communal memory."[8] Many of these future-prophets seemed to focus their attention on the year 2000, when their predictions should come to pass.

These kind of predictions were obviously inaccurate and in obvious need of qualification and modification to what actually was taking place by the end of the century. Martha Boaz wrote a more realistic assessment in 1987, stating that:

> A point to remember...is that, due to the progress of technology, materials needed on a very current, up-to-date basis are put into media form that is faster than the printed pages. For this reason, books are becoming less important in the fields of science and technology, and although the traditional library will continue to exist, there will be and already are different requirements for it in certain areas. Methods of acquiring library materials, for accessioning them, for storing and for servicing them are being provided through high speed facsimile, reproduction, and communication devices., There will be more microforms and computer-based data banks.[9]

Hence, a more accurate appraisal, or clearer focus in terms of the impact of the electronic age by the end of the 20th century, would be that it resulted in the growing computerization of the library world, as well as the entire realm of information, thus facilitating access to information on a global scale. By the close of the century predictions about the electronic/information age no longer focused on the year 2000, but now shifted to projections about the first quarter of the next century. In essay dealing with the 21st century Maurice B. Line described libraries in 2015 as follows:

> Printed books and journals will then still exist alongside a variety of electronic media that can be acquired and online access to much material. Information media, whether available in printed or electronic form, will need to be kept and made available somewhere, and libraries (or whatever they are called in A.D. 2015) will continue to serve this function; there is no other sort of body equally fitted to do so, and it would be pointless to

invent one. Libraries will thus continue to serve as collections of information resources...[10]

Although the basic function of libraries will, hence, continue to remain the same, how it goes about fulfilling that task will evolve. Among the concepts which will, and are undergoing change is that of ownership. Bart Harloe and John Budd maintain that "where once-upon a time academic research libraries pursued the proud goal of a comprehensive stand alone collection of resources that would meet most (if not all) needs of local patrons. It is now necessary to begin the collective migration to a more streamlined, post-modern collection of collections/mediated by new electronic networking technology that connects scholars across space and time. In other words, economic forces and technological advances have combined together to create a new environment, one where access to collective scholarly resources that no one library could ever afford superseded the historic quest for the great comprehensive collection.[11]

In November 1996, the Benton Foundation at the request of the W.K. Kellog Foundation published *Buildings, Books, and Bytes*, a report which indicates what library leaders and the general public in the U.S. think about the future of libraries in the digital age. The report concludes that libraries are "at a crossroads, for they must adjust their traditional values and services to the digital age. But there is good reason for optimism as libraries and their communities take up this challenge. Libraries have enormous opportunities nationwide to influence and direct public opinion because strong public sentiment already supports key visions for the future of libraries. Moreover, the growing use of home computers seems, at least at this juncture, to complement not compete with library use. So libraries and their leaders must chart a role for themselves, giving meaning and message to their future institutions and their central role in community life."

Finally, a word should be said about the value of library history: As the future development of libraries and information in general becomes a topic of increasing interest, it is important to view and place these developments in historical context. Indeed, Library History can provide the foundation to an understanding for future developments. Jesse Shera has noted that those with an understanding of historical origins will be better equipped to deal with the developments of the future, observing that the degree of success "will be largely determined by the extent to which practical considerations are founded upon historic truth...history is not an esoteric or special branch of knowledge but a synthesis of life itself." He also observes that history is not an occasional or partial affair but that point of intersection where past and future meet.[12]

In his *History of Libraries of the Western World* (1995), Michael H. Harris, has noted the importance of library history as it relates to future developments, observing that "the library has played a vital cultural role in societies all over the world, and we are now coming to understand the extent to which the library is an institution embedded in the cultural realm of society, and the extent to which its structural and functional characteristics are determined by its definition as an institution contrived to consume, preserve, transmit, and reproduce the history of civilization." And he advises that "all who would predict the future of libraries would be wise to attend to the long history of library and information services in the past."

Several observations which Henry Petroski makes in his book, *The Book on the Bookshelf* (1999) dealing with the historical aspects of books, shelving, and libraries, are also relevant to a consideration of the value of library history. He writes that: "These are not arcane subjects that have little relevance for the new millennium; they are among the basic data of civilization that provide a means to a better understanding of the evolving technology of today and to extrapolating it into the future, which will be more like the present and the past than we are usually led to believe."

The basic data, the building blocks and foundations of civilization—these are the contributions that libraries have provided throughout the ages, and to understand this continuum is perhaps one of the best available guides to future developments in the world of libraries.

NOTES FOR THE PREFACE AND INTRODUCTION

Preface

[1] Alfred Hessel, *Geschichte der Bibliotheken: Ein Überblick von ihren Anfängen bis zur Gegenwart.* (Göttingen: Hochschulbuchverlag, 1925).
[2] Alfred Hessel and Reuben Peiss, *A History of Libraries.* (Metuchen, NJ: Scarecrow Pr., 1950).

Introduction

[1] Paal Raabe, *Library History and the History of Books—Two Fields of Research for Librarians*, in: *Essays in Honor of James Edward Walsh. On His Sixty-Fifth Birthday.* (Cambridge, Mass: The Goethe Institute and the Houghton Library, 1983), p.9.
[2] Oscar Handlin, *Truth in History.* (Cambridge, Mass: The Belknap Press of Harvard University Pr., 1979), p.405–06.
[3] Francis Lieber cited in: Michael H. Harris, ed., *Reader in American Library History.* (Washington, D.C.: NCR Microcard Editions, 1971), p.201.
[4] Raabe, p.15.

NOTES FOR THE CHAPTERS

Chapter I.

[1] Fritz Milkau *Geschichte der Bibliotheken im alten Orient* (Liepzig, 1935), a scholarly survey of pre-Alexandrian libraries with copious bibliographical notes giving an evaluation of the literature, is unfortunately not available in English translation. J.W. Thompson, *Ancient Libraries* (Berkeley, 1940) is useful chiefly for bibliography. Frederick Kenyon, *Books and Readers in Ancient Greece and Rome* (London, 1935) is short, authoritative, and stimulating.
[2] "Die Bibliothek...war nach sachlichen Gruppen wohl geordnet und mit Orientierungsmarken versehen." J. Menant, *La bibliothèque du palais de Ninève* (Paris, 1880), p.32 states flatly: "A careful examination of the inscriptions shows that they were arranged in the library in a methodical order easy to reconstruct." Carl

Bezold, however, after painstaking study, contents himself, in the *Catalogue of the Cuneiform Tablets in the Kouynunjik Collection of the British Museum*, V (London 1889), p.xxix, with: "We have no knowledge as to the way in which the tablets were arranged in Ashur-bani-pal's Library." That there was some sort of systematic arrangement is a matter of general agrement. Many of the tablets clearly belong to series; the order of each tablet within the series is often indicated at its beginning by a repetition of the last line of the preceding tablet, and, at the end of the first line of the tablet which follows. There are also tablets bearing series titles, and references to the series or group to which a tablet belongs sometimes appear in the colophon. The study of this library is still far from complete. Ci. R.C. Thompson and R.W. Hutchinson, *A Century of Exploration at Nineveh* (London, 1929) for a brief but expert survey. Edward Chiera, *They Wrote on Clay* (Chicago, 1938) is a sprightly general introduction to cuneiform tablets and their historical significance.

[3] The term used in most Western languages derives from the compounding of two Greek words: biblos, book and theke, container or repository.

[4] Aristophanes, *Frogs*, 943, 1409. Cf. also Athenaeus, Deipnosophistae, I,3: "Euripides possessed one of the largest libraries in the ancient world."

[5] For descriptions and illustrations of the layout of ancient libraries see Bernt Götze, "Antike Bibliotheken," *Jahrbuch des deutschen archäologischen Institutes*, III (1937), 225–247.

[6] Graetia capta jerum victorem cepit. Horace, *Epistles*, II, I, 156.

[7] See Felix Reichmann, "The Book Trade at the Time of the Roman Empire," *Library Quarterly*, VIII (1938), 40–76.

[8] Primus ingenia hominum rem publicam fecit. Pliny, *Naturalis Historia*, XXXV, 10.

[9] For a sketch of the libraries of Rome see C.E. Boyd, *Public Libraries and Literary Culture in Ancient Rome* (Chicago, 1916).

[10] For a description of such a library see H.F. Pfeiffer, "Roman Library at Timgad," *Memoirs of the American Academy in Rome* IX (1931), 157–165.

[11] Iam enim inter balnearia et thermas bibliotheca quoque ut necessarium domus ornamentum expolitur. —Seneca, *De tranquillitate animi* IX, 4.

[12] Quo innumerabiles libros et bibliothecas, quorum dominus vix tota vita indices perlegit. —Ibid. IX, 7.

[13] See Götze, op. cit.

Chapter II.

[1] The period covered in the next four chapters is dealt with in great detail in J.W. Thompson, *The Medieval Library* (Chicago, 1939). This is the latest and most comprehensive treatment in English, but it must be read with some caution. C.P. Farrar and A.P. Evans, *Bibliography of English Trnaslations from Medieval Sources* (New York, 1946) provides a useful guide to the literature of the period. Falconer Madan, *Books in Manuscript* (2nd ed. London, 1927) is a little classic in its field.

[2] *Ammianus Macellinus*, XIV, 6, 18.

3 Si quem sancta tenet meditandi in lege voluntas Hic poterit residens sacris intendere libris.

4 See Cardinal Gasquet's translation, *The Rule of Saint Benedict* (London, 1925).

5 *Isidori Opera Omnia* (Rome) 1803), VII, 179. Quoted in J.W. Clark, *The Care of Books* (Cambridge, 1909), p.46.

6 Bibliothecarius ominum librorum curam habeat, lectionum et scriptorum. Cf. C. Cipolla *Codice diplomatico del monasterio di S. Columbano di Bobbio*, I (Rome, 1918), p.140.

7 For an account of Bede and the monasteries of Wearmouth and Jarrow see *Bede: His Life, Times, and Writings; Essays in Commemoration of the Twelfth Centenary of his Death*, ed. by Alexander H. Thompson (Oxford, 1935).

8 Emil Lesne, *Les livres, "scriptoria," et bibliotheques du commencement du viiie a la fin du xie siecle* (Lille, 1938) is an admirable study, chiefly of France, but including also some libraries now within the national boundaries of Germany and Switzerland.

9 A helpful little study of Alcuin and his work is A.F. West, *Alcuin and the Rise of Christian Schools* (New York, 1892).

10 Quis saltem poterit seriem enumerare librorum Quos tua de multis copulat sententia terris.—*Monumenta Germaniae historica. Poetae latini medii aevi*, I, 96.

Chapter III.

1 Hae ergo divitiae claustrales, hae sunt opulentiae caelestis vitae dulcedine animam saginantes. —From the catalogue of the monastery of St. Riquier, reprinted in E. Edwards, *Memoirs of Libraries...*I, 297-301.

2 Inexplicabilis librorum copia periit, nosque spiritualium nostri armorum inarmes reliquit.—I have been unable to identify this passage.

3 Claustrum sine armario quasi castrum sine armentario.—Geoffrey of St. Barbe in *Thesaurus novus anecdotorum*, ed. E. Marté and U. Durand (Paris, 1717), I, 511.

4 Quidquid ab arce deus coeli direxit in orbem Scripturae sanctae per pia verba viris, Illic invenies, quidquid sapientia mundi, Protulit in mundum temporibus variis. — "Hrabani Mauri Carmina XIII: Ad Gerhohum Prestiberum," in *Monumenta Germaniae historica. Poetae latini medii aevi*, II, 187.

5 See Joan Evans, *Monastic Life at Cluny, 910-1157* (London, 1931). For France in general, see Lesne, op. cit.

6 See J.S. Beddie, "The Ancient Classics in the Medieval Libraries," *Speculum,* V (1930), 3-20, and his "Libraries in the 12th Century,

7 In this connection see the informative and entertaining chapter by Florence E. de Roover, "The Scriptorium," in J.W. Thompson, *The Midieval Library*.

8 Hoc ut nullus opus cuiquam concesserit extra, Ni prius ille fidem dederit vel denique pignus,, Donec ad has ades, quae accepit, salva remittat. —Quoted by W. Wattenbach, *Das Schriftwesen im Mittelalter* (3rd. ed. Leipzig, 1896), p.572.

9 See Dorothy M. Norris, *A History of Cataloguing and Cataloguing Methods* (London, 1939).

Chapter IV.

[1] The standard work in English on medieval universities is Hastings Rashdall, *The Universities of Europe in the Middle Ages* (New ed. Oxford, 1936). A shorter and more popular account is Nathan Schachner, *The Mediaeval Universities* (New York and London, 1938).

[2] The reference is apparently to Gabriel Meier, *Heinrich von Ligerz, Bibliothekar von Einsiedeln im 14. Jahrhundert* (Leipzig, 1896).

[3] An association of reformed Benedictine Monks.

[4] See Norris, op. cit., 30-34.

[5] See Ruth S. Mackensen, "Four Great Libraries of Medieval Baghdad," *Library Quarterly*, II (1932), 279-299. See also the chapter contributed by S.K.Padover to J.W. Thompson's *The Medieval Library*, which gives additional references.

[6] "Audivit...de quodam Sarracenorum soldano quod omnia librorum genera, quae nicessaria esse poterant philosophis Sarracenis diligenter faciebat inquiri, et sumptibus suis scribi, et in armario suo recondi, ut litterati eorum liborum copiam possent habere, quoties indigerent." Geoffroy de Beaulieu, Vita Ludovici Noni, XXIII *(Recueil des historiens des Gaules et de la France*, XX 91840), 15).

[7] La belle librarie...de tous les plus notables volumes, qui par souverains auteurs aient estés compilés...de toutes sciences, moult bien escrips et richment adornez. — Quoted in Léopold Delisle, *Recherches sur la librairie de Charles V* (Paris, 1907), I,2.

[8] The library was bought by the Duke of Bedford in 1424 and removed to England.

[9] See the historical introduction by J.W. Thompson to *The Frankfort Book Fair* (Chicago, 1911), a translation of Henri Estienne's *Francofordiense Emporium*.

[10] See the works by Rashdall and Schachner already cited.

[11] A detailed study of this arrangement, with helpful illustrations, is B.H. Streeter; *The Chained Library* (London, 1931).

Chapter V.

[1] So far as I can discover there exists no complete English translation of this work other than an early one by Thomas Twyne, *Phisicke against Fortune, as well prosperous as adverse*

[2] Libri medullitus delectant, colloquuntur, consulunt et viva quandam nobis atque arguta familiaritate junguntur. - Letter to Giovanni d'Incisa. See Petrarca, Le Familiare, ed. *Vittorio Rossi* (Florence, 1932-1941), I, 139.

[3] One of the greatest of fifteenth-century private libraries is described in Pearl Kibre, *The Library of Pico della Mirandola* (New York, 1936).

[4] ad ingeniosorum et nobilium, quos continget in talibus delectari, consolationem. The legacy is printed in P. Nolhac, *Pétrarque et l'humanisme* (new ed. Paris, 1907), I, 94.

[5] It is impossible to reproduce in English the allusion so neatly struck off by the German "Börsenblatt." The *Börsenblatt* is is the regular organ of the German book trade. The nearest American analogy is *Publishers' Weekly*.

[6] A translation, "Plautus in the Convent," has been published in v.14 of the collection *German Classics of the Nineteenth Century*, ed. by Kuno Francke.

7 "Memioni Constantinopoli Graeculis illis vestimenta dedisse, ut codices acciperem, cuius rei nec pudet nec poenitat." Carteggio di Giovanni Aurispa, a cura di remigio Sabbadini (Rome, 1931), p.91.

8 R. Sabbadini, *Le scoperte dei codici latini e greci ne secoli* xiv e xv, I, 164.

9 "docto, de bono aspecto, de bona natura, et bona et expedita lingua." C. Stornajolo, *Codices Urbinates Graeci Bibliothecae Vaticanae* (Rome, 1895), I, Praef.XX.

10 For a sketch of this library's history see Geza Schütz, Bibliotheca Corvina," *Library Quarterly* IV (1934), 552-564.

11 "When Cosimo de Medici wanted to provide the Monastery of Saint Mark in Florence, which he had built, with a library, he prevailed upon the then highly regarded book expert, Tomaso de Sarzana, to draw up a standard catalogue from which purchases could begin to be made. Later, when Tomaso himself had become Pope, his catalogue spread far and wide under the title, The Inventory of Pope Nicholas V, Which he Composed at the Request of Cosimo de Medici himself, and in scope and arrangement it served as a model for the setting up of new libraries. It began with the Bible as the comprehensive and the most important work on theology, followed by the Church Fathers. After the theologians, as a second division, come the philosophers, beginning, as is proper, with Aristotle. The humanities form the third division, and the classic poets occupy the chief place. The fourth division, jurisprudence, as chance would have it, is missing in the copy of the inventory that has come down to us, but as we have seen from the foregoing description of the Library of Urbino, which was arranged according to this inventory, that section was originally present in the inventory."—Translated from Franz Wickhoff, "Die Bibliothek Julius' II," *Jahrbuch der preussißchen Kunstsammlungen* XIV (1893), 53-54. A copy of the inventory is published in G. Sforza, La patria, *la famiglia e la giovinessa di Papa Niccolo V* (Lucca, 1884), Appendix A.

12 Di libri antiqui...per public' uso, Sisto da tutto il mondo fe' raccorre. Ariosto, "Satira VI (VII)," 139-141 in his Opere Minori, ed. *Seven Famous Discourses...in English* by Garius Markham (London, 1708).

13 The paintings in the Stanza della Segnatura, then, provide us with a pictorial representation of a book catalogue, a project which is rather remarkable in a room designed to be used for everyday purposes...The allegorical figures which sit enthroned on high have books in their hands; only Justice has her hands full with sword and scales. The Gospels, the books most revered by Christians, are being brought down to the faithful by angels; and four Holy Fathers gathered about the sacrament are writing and reading books; books are scattered about the ground, and saints and laymen in the company are distinguished by posessing them; those who rejoice in the mysterious presence of the Muse hold rolls and manuscripts; books and tablets are in everybody's hands in the School of Athens. Composing, copying, reading, expounding books goes on in all corners,so that hardly any conceivable relation to books fails to find here a sensible expression. Even the two greatest of the philosophers are only indicated by their two most famous books; the Pope holds a book along with the laws of the Church, and Justinian is seated with his famous Corpus before him. On the cameos below the Parnassus, on one side books are found in a marble sarcophagus, on the other, books are being burned. There exists no other work of painting in

which books play so large a role, in which everything starts from and returns to books."—Translated from Franz Wickhoff, loc. cit.

[14] There is a considerable body of literature on Italy's influence on Chaucer, but little is known, apparently, about his use of Italian libraries. See R.A. Pratt, "Chaucer and the Visconti Libraries," *ELH: A Journal of English Literary History*, VI (1939), 191-200.

[15] There is a thoroughgoing study of this influence in German: Heinrich Kramm, *Deutsche Bibliotheken unter dem Einfluss von Humanismus und Reformation* (Leipzig, 1938).

Chapter VI.

[1] "An die Ratherren aller Stadte deutsches Lands." The letter is translated in Chapter IX of F.V.N. Painter's *Luther on Education* (Philadelphia, 1890). I have used Painter's translation of this passage.

[2] James Brodrick has now given us a detailed account of these activities in his *St. Peter Canisius* (London, 1935). The concluding chapter contains a resume of Canisius' accomplishments in education.

[3] So called from the collection of books bound in silver which came from Anna Marie, the second wife of Duke Albert of Prussia.

[4] "Ist auch allzeit gewesen Weisheit und Kunst geneigt". Quoted by Hans Rott, *Ott Heinrich und die Kunst* (Heidelberg, 1905), p.173. (*Mitteilungen zur Geschichte des Heidelberger Schlosses* V, 1/2).

[5] nonulla quibus ingenua curiositas hominis eruditi delectari solet, tanquam proprio pastu animi liberalis, als da seien instrumenta mathematica, numismata antiqua, erudita rudera prisci temporis sowie quaedam naturae et artis miracula.—Cf. C. Clement, *Musei sive bibliothecae tam privatae quam publicae extructio, instruction, cura, usus* (Lyon, 1635), p.376.

[6] For an account of Gesner which amiably denies to him the honor of founder see T. Besterman, *The Beginnings of Systematic Bibliography* (2nd ed. London, 1936). Archer Taylor, in his useful little *Renaissance Guides to Books* (Berklley, 1945), agrees with Besterman in dating modern bibliography from Johannes Tritheim (1462-1516).

[7] There is an English translation by John Evelyn, *Instructions concerning Erecting of a Library* (London, 1661) reprinted Cambridge, 1903. See also J.V. Rice, *Gabriel Naudé, 1600-1653* (Baltimore, 1939)

[8] See Gabriel Naudé, News from France, or a Description of the Library of Cardinal Mazarin, preceded by *The Surrender of the Library* (Chicago, 1907). Cf. Also, J.V. Rice, *Gabriel Naudé, 1600-1653* (Baltimore, 1939).

[9] See *Trecentale Bodleianum: a Memorial Volume for the Three Hundredth Anniversary of the Public Funeral of Sir Thomas Bodley* (Oxford, 1913).

[10] Je vis la bibliothèque sans nulle difficulté, chacun la voit einsin et en extrait ce qu'il veut. —Montaigne, *Journal de voyage en Italie par la Suisse et l'Allemagne en 1580 et 1581, ed. Maurice Rat* (Paris, 1942), p.114. There are several English translations.

[11] Sum de bibliotheca quam Heidelberga capta spolium fecit et Gregorio XV trophaeum misit Maximilianus dux Bavariae.

[12] Medios inter praeliorum strepitus, victoriarum curcum. Quoted by A. Hortzchansky, *Die Königliche Bibliothek zu Berlin* (Berlin, 1908), p.19.

Chapter VII.

[1] See Martha Ornstein, *The Role of Scientific Societies in the Seventeenth Century* (Chicago, 1928).

[2] See J.N. Bergkamp, *Dom Jean Mabillon and the Benedictine Historical School of Saint-Maur* (Washington, D.C., 1928).

[3] Monsieur Colbert n'oublie rien de ce qu'il faut pour augmenter et embellir la bibliothèque afin de contenter la genereuse inclination de son maître. —I have been unable to verify this quotation.

[4] *Des Deviors et des qualités du bibliothecaire.* The English translation (Chicago, 1906) has a brief bibliographical introduction.

[5] Spartitio universalis doctrinae humanae. It is interesting to note that after the War of 1812, when the Library of Congress was reconstituted out of Jefferson's private collection, the classification it used was Jefferson's adaption of Bacon's scheme.

[6] A great collection of archives and historical documents now known as the Collection Moreau from the name of the Parisian lawyer who instigated it. See Henri Omont, *La Collection Moreau* (Paris, 1891).

[7] Not only religious images, but many books too, were destroyed as a result of religious controversy in seventeenth-century England. See C.R. Gillett, Burned Books (New York, 1932).

[8] Cf. W.E. Axon, "An Italian Librarian of the XVII and XVIII Centuries, Antonio Magliabechi," *Library Association Record V* (1903), 59-76.

[9] Founded in 1770. At first a military academy only, it developed into a general university. In 1794 it was dissolved by Duke Louis Eugene of Wurttemberg.

[10] The Communist revolution was epoch-making for this, as for all Russian libraries. For a brief account, see Chapter IX.

[11] See further A.L. Clarke, "Leibniz as a Librarian," *The Library III*, ser.5 (1914), 140-154.

[12] Non modo scientia bibliothecariorum omnium longe princeps erat, sed etiam elegentissima humanitate et exprompta adversus hospites facilitate. J.A. Ernesti, *Narratio de Ionne Matthia Gesnero...*(Leipzig, 1826), p.30.

Chapter VIII.

[1] See Charles Mortet, "The Public Libraries of France, National, Communal, and University," *Library Association Record,* n.s. vol.III (1925), 145-159. Important French library laws of the eighteenth and nineteenth centuries will be found in Ulysse Robert, Recueil de lois, décrets, ordonnances, arrêtés, circulaires, etc. concernant les biblithèques publiques, communales, universitaires, scolaires et populaires (Paris, 1883). Se also Christian de Serres de Mesplès, *Les bibliothèques publiques francaises—leur organization—leur reform* (Montpellier, 1933).

2 See Henri Lemaître, *Histoire du dépôt légal. Ire partie* (Paris, 1910); Robert Crouzel, *Le dépôt légal* (Toulouse, 1936).

3 The Imperial Deputation, composed of eight influential political leaders of the German Empire, effected a drastic territorial redistribution which greatly reduced the number of autonomous units within the empire and abolished almost all the ecclesiastical states, imperial villages, and free cities. "The net result of the redistribution was to build up a number of medium-sized states with some approach to geographical homogeneity."—C.T. Atkinson, *A History of Germany, 1715-1815* (London, 1908), p. 460.

4 Although the university library has a considerable reference collection of its own, it has always been able to fall back upon the vast scholarly resources of the Prussian State Library, with which it therefore does not try to compete.

5 Attention should be called, however, to the printed subject indexes of the British Museum: *Subject Index of the Modern Works added to the Library, 1881* (London, 1902-); and *Subject Index of Books Published up to and including 1880. Series 1-3* (London, 1933-1939).

6 *Catalogus codicum manuscriptorum Bibliothecae regiae monacensis.* Tom. I-III. (Munich, 1858-1915).

7 This has been translated into English by Arthur Browne with the title *A General Bibliographical Dictionary, from the German of Frederic Adolphus Ebert.* (Oxford, 1837).

8 Ueber öffentliche Bibliotheken. I have been unable to find an English translation. The term "public library" here should be taken to mean "library open to public use" as over against the private library. More will be said further on concerning the kinds of public libraries in Germany.

9 *Die Bildung des Bibliothekars.* There is an English translation (Woodstock, Vt., 1916).

10 See C.F. Gosnell and Geza Schütz, "Goethe the Librarian," *Library Quarterly II*, (1932), 367-374. A fuller account can be found in Otto Lerche, *Goethe und die Weimarer Bibliothek* (Leipzig, 1929).

11 Control of German university libraries in the nineteenth century was commonly in the hands of a committee composed of officials such as the rector and the deans and members of the several faculties of instruction. In order to achieve recognition and true responsibility the professional librarian had to emancipate himself from overly rigid supervision by this committee.

12 Cobbett's words are worth quoting at some length: "Let those who lounged in it, and made it a place of amusement, contribute to its support. Why should tradesmen and farmers be called upon to pay for the support of a place which was intended only for the amusement of the curious and the rich, and not for the benefit or the instruction of the poor? If the aristocracy wanted the Museum as a lounging place, let them pay for it." *Hansard's Parliamentary Debates*, ser.3, vol XVI (March 1 - April 1, 1833), p.1003.

13 Cf. R.C.B. Partridge, *The History of the Legal Deposit of Books Throughout the British Empire* (London, 1938).

14 The printing of this catalogue continues. It was expected that it would be completed shortly after 1940, but the outbreak of war in 1939 upset this plan. E.G. Ledos,

Histoire des catalogues des livres imprimés de la Bibliothèque Nationale (Paris, 1936) provides a detailed expert account of the various catalogues of printed books of this great library, and the admirable preface by M. Julien Cain, administrateur général of the library, gives a brief historical survey of its cataloguing procedures.

[15] *Die Selbstandigkeit des bibliothekarischen Berufes.* The pamphlet has not been translated.

[16] Arnold Sachse, Friedrich Althoff und sein Werk (Berlin, 1928) now fills the gap which existed when this sentence was written. Out of some 350 pages it devotes some 10 to Althoff's library activities, but many of these activities connect with, and flow from, wider educational accomplishments, to which a good deal of space is given. See also Friedrich Schmidt-Ott, "Althoff und die Bibliotheken," Zentralblatt für Bibliothekswesen LVI (1939), 101-103.

[17] See F.E. Hirsch, "The Scholar as Librarian; to the Memory of Adolf von Harnack," Library Quarterly IX (1939), 299-320.

[18] *Jahresverzeichnis der an den deutschen Universitäten erschienenen Schriften.*

[19] *Bibliographischer Monatsbericht über neu erschienenen Schul-, Universitäts- und Hochschulschriften.*

[20] *Berliner Titeldrucke.* For a brief sketch of the history of this publication, see the introduction to The Prussian Instructions ... Translated by Andrew D. Osborn (Ann Arbor, 1938).

[21] The *Deutscher Gesamtkatalog,* begun in 1931 as the *Gesamtkatalog der preussischen Bibliotheken,* was designed to give this information in printed form. So far only 14 volumes (carrying the alphabet as far as the middle of the letter B) have appeared.

[22] E.H. Vouilléme, *Die Inkunabeln der Königlichen Bibliothek und der anderen Berliner Sammlungen* (Leipzig, 1906).

Chapter IX.

[1] For the more recent history of these institutions see Arundell Esdaile, "Between Two Wars in the British Museum," Library Quarterly XII (1942), 794-804; and José Meyer, "The Bibliothèque Nationale During the Last Decade," ibid, 805-826. It is probably too early to assess the effects of World War II on these libraries.

[2] See the painstaking account by David C. Mearns, *The Story up to Now* (Washington, 1948).

[3] Cf. Essays Offered to Herbert Putnam by his Colleagues and Friends on his Thirtieth Anniversary as Librarian of Congress, 5 April 1929 (New Haven, 1929).

[4] For further details see Lucy Salamanca, *Fortress of Freedom* (Philadelphia, 1942).

[5] The first supplement, published in 1948, contains printed cards issued from August 1, 1942 through December 31, 1947. Cards printed after that date are contained in the *Cumulative Catalog of Library of Congress Printed Cards* (Washington, 1947-)

[6] First printed in the *Library Quarterly XIV* (1944), 277-315, and reprinted in the *Annual Report of the Librarian of Congress for ... 1945* (Washington, D.C.), p.107-142.

[7] What happened to this library during, and immediately after, the war is described in Richard S. Hill, "The Former Prussian State Library," *Music Library Association Notes III* (1945-46), 327-350, 404-410.

8 For a preliminary estimate of the destruction see George Leyh, "Die Lage der deutschen wissenschaftlichen Bibliotheken nach dem Kriege," *Zentralblatt für Bibliothekswesen LXI* (1947), 19-32.

9 For a list of the more important bibliographical publications of the Deutsche Bücherei see Otto Neuburger, *Official Publications of Present-Day Germany* (Washington, D.C., 1942), p.61-62. The Soviet Military Administration has granted permission for resumption of publication of these bibliographies. In 1946 the *Deutsche Nationalbibliographie* reappeared, and preparations are being made to produce some of the other titles as soon as possible. A new post-war bibliography resembling the *Deutsche Nationalbibliographie* and listing primarily publications of the British, French, and American zones of occupied Germany is the *Bibliographie der Deutschen Bibliothek,* Frankfurt a.M.

10 Central control has been strengthened after the recent war by decrees appointing M. Julien Cain director of the libraries of France, and giving to the director wide powers. See *Journal officiel de la République française*, 24 August 1945, p.5293 and 13 March 1946, p.2119.

11 See the *Survey of Losses and Needs of Libraries in Some European Countries put out by the Preparatory Commission of the United Nations Educational, Scientific and Cultural Organization* (UNESCO Prep. Com/L&M/13. App. I. Paris, November 14, 1946. Mimeographed).

12 This has been asserted on a very small scale, however, with the result that there is still much variety among French municipal libraries.

13 See I. Giordani, "The Work of Italian Libraries," *Library Quarterly* VIII (1938), 145-155.

14 *Norme per il catalogo degli stampati*, 2nd ed. (Città del Vaticano, 1939). An English edition, *Rules for the Catalog of Printed Books*, translated by T.J. Shanahan, V.A. Shaefer, and C.T. Vesselowsky, and edited by W.E. Wright, was published in 1948.

15 See E. Tisserant, "The Preparation of a Main Index for the Vatican Library Manuscripts," in *William Warner Bishop; a Tribute*, 1941, p.176-185. For information on Bishop, see Claud Glenn Sparks, *Doyen of Librarians: A Biography of William Warner Bishop.* (Metuchen, NJ: Scarecrow Press, 1993).

16 See *Fünfzig Jahre Schweizerische Landesbibliothek, 1895-1945*, (Bern, 1945).

17 Dans les Etats-Unis l'ensemble de l'éducation des hommes est dirigé vers la politique.

18 Sidney Ditzion, *Arsenals of a Democratic Culture: A Social History of the American Public Library Movement in New England and the Middle States from 1850 to 1900* (Chicago, 1947) makes a good beginning in this field. A major contribution to the history of the public library movement in New England is: Jesse H. Shera, *Foundations of the Public Library* (Chicago, 1949)

19 See B.C. Steiner, ed., *Rev. Thomas Bray; his Life and Selected Works Relating to Maryland* (Baltimore, 1901); W.D. Houlette, {Parish Libraries and the Work of the Reverend Thomas Bray," *Library Quarterly* IV (1934), 588-609.

20 C.B. Joeckel, *The Government of the American Public Library* (Chicago, 1935), p.111-150 et passim.

21 For a sketch of Billings' qualities and manifold achievements see H.M. Lydenberg, *John Shaw Billings* (Chicago, 1924).

22 A good idea of the complex functions of a large public library can be obtained from the annual report of the New York Public Library. For a detailed description of the Chicago Public Library see C.B. Joeckel and L. Carnovsky, *A Metropolitan Library in Action* (Chicago, 1940). The clearest picture of the role played in the community by the average American public library will be found in R.S. and H.M. Lynd, *Middletown* (New York, 1929) and *Middletown in Transition* (New York, 1937).

23 Cf. Sidney Ditzion, "The Anglo-American Library Scene: A Contribution to the Social History of the Library Movement," *Library Quarterly* XVI (1946), 281-301.

24 For further details see J. Minto, *A History of the Public Library Movement in Great Britain and Ireland* (London, 1932).

25 L.R. McColvin, *The Public Library System of Great Britain* (London, 1942).

26 See further, A. Arnesen, "How Norway Became the Focus of American Library Methods in Europe." *Library Quarterly* IV (1934), 148-155. It is also worth noting that one of the most acute works on American libraries has been written by a Norwegian: W. Munthe, *American Librarianship from a European Angle* (Chicago, 1939).

27 W. Schuster, "Die Zusammenarbeit der Stadtbibliothek mit den Volksbüchereien," *Zentralblatt für Bibliothekswesen* LV (1938), 457-467.

28 There have been several changes of title. Its last title was *Die Bücherei* and it was published by the Government Bureau for Popular Library Affairs (Reichsstelle für Volksbüchereiwesen). It ceased publication shortly before the end of World War II.

29 See W. Scheffen, "Zwanzig Jahre 'Grenzbüchereidienst', *Die Bücherei* VII (1940), 254-263.

30 It is interesting to note, however, that the first library journal to be published in Germany after the war was devoted to popular libraries: *Der Volksbibliothekar* (Berlin, I, No. 1. Oct., 1946-). Publication was aided and encouraged by the Soviet Military Administrations.

31 There is no English term which exactly gives the sense of the German. "Einheitsbibliothek," as nearly as we can translate it, means "unified library," that is a library in which a number of functions are now performed in a central place which formerly were performed in disparate libraries of a special type—either scholarly or popular.

32 These figures are, of course, pre-war. Both libraries may well have been demolished during the fighting.

33 *The Handbook of Medical Library Practice*, (Chicago, 1943), produced by the Medical Library Association, lists the largest medical libraries in the world in Chapter I, Appendix I. From the figures there presented it transpires that the three largest medical libraries—and twelve of the thirty-six largest—are in the Soviet Union.

34 See D.M. Krassovsky, "Bibliographical Work In Russia," *Library Quarterly* IV (1934), 449-466; A.B. Berthold, "Survey of Recent Russian Library Literature," *Library Quarterly* XVII (1947), 138-147; N. Delougaz, "Some Problems of Soviet Librarianship as Reflected in Russian Library Periodicals," *Library Quarterly* XV (1945), 213-223.

German Collections of the Library of Congress: Chronological Development. (Washington, D.C.: The Library of Congress, 1994).

[3] For a history of OCLC, see Anne Marie Allison and Ann Allan, eds., *OCLC: A National Library Network.* (Short Hills, NJ: Enslow Publishers, 1979).

[4] See Michael H. Harris and Stanley Hannah, *The Foundations of Library and Information Services in the Post-Industrial Era.* (Norwood, NJ: Ablex. 1992).

[5] S.H. Steinberg, *Five Hundred Years of Printing*, Third Edition. (Harmondsworth, Eng.: Penguin Books, 1974), p.11.

[6] Marshall McLuhan, *The Gutenberg Galaxy: The Making of Typographic Man.* (New York: New American Library, 1962).

[7] F. Wilfrid Lancaster, *The Impact of a Paperless Society on the Research Library of the Future.* (Champaign-Urbana, Ill,: Library Research Center, Graduate School of Library Science, University of Illinois, 1980).

[8] James Thompson, *The End of Libraries.* (London: C. Bingeley, 1982).

[9] Martha Boaz, *Librarian/Library Educator: An Autobiography and Planning for the Future.* (Metuchen, NJ: Scarecrow Pr., 1987).

[10] Maurice B. Line, "Libraries and Information Services in 25 Years' Time: A British Perspective," in: F.W. Lancaster, ed., *Libraries and the Future: Essays on the Library in the Twenty-First Century.* (New York: Haworth Pr., 1993), p.77.

[11] Bart Harloe and John Budd, "Collection, Development and Scholarly Communication in the Era of Electronic Access," *The Journal of Academic Librarianship.* 18:3-4 (1992-93):83.

[12] Jesse Shera as cited in: Michael H. Harris, ed., *Reader in American Library History.* (Washington, D.C.: Microcard Editions, 1971), p.13.

SELECTIVE BIBLIOGRAPHY

References to works dealing with topics discussed in the text can be found in the footnotes. Guides to works dealing with library history in general and American library history in particular are listed as follows:

1. GENERAL WORKS:

An excellent basic guide to library history can be found in: Wayne E. Wiegand and Donald G. Davis, *Encyclopedia of Library History.* (New York: Garland, 1994). This provides encyclopedia coverage to a wide range of various aspects of the field. For an annual review of publications dealing with library and book history, see *ABHB: Annual Bibliography of the History of the Printed Book and Libraries* (The Hague: Nijhoff, 1970-). For recent research in the field, see *Libraries & Culture: A Journal of Library History* (Austin, Texas: University of Texas Press).

Among general histories, the following is especially valuable: Michael H. Harris, *History of Libraries in the Western World.* Fourth edition. (Metuchen, NJ: Scarecrow Press, 1995). Also, see his essay "History of the Library," *Encyclopedia Americana.* 17(1995): 311-25. For a more recent survey, see: Fred Lerner, *The Story of Libraries: From the Invention of Writing to the Computer Age.* (New York: Continuum, 1998).

2. AMERICAN LIBRARY HISTORY:

For a guide to American library history in particular, see Donald G. Davis, Jr. and John Mark, *American Library History: A Comprehensive Guide.* (Santa Barbara, CA: ABC-CLIO, 1989), and for more recent publications consult "The Year's Work in American Library History," published in the journal, *Libraries & Culture,* previously, *Journal of Library History.* Biographical information can be found in Wayne E. Wiegand, *Dictionary of American Library Biography.* (Littleton, COLO: Libraries Unlimited, 1978), and a basic chronological history in Elizabeth Stone, *American Library Development, 1600-1899.* (New York: H.W. Wilson, 1977). Also see, Michael H. Harris, ed., *Reader in American Library History.* (Washington, D. C.: NCR, 1971).

3. WEBSITES:

A number of websites are available, which relate to Library History, but the two most important are:

- The Round Table on Library History <http://ifla.inist.fr/VII/rt8/rtlh.htm>

This is maintained by the Round Table of the Section of Library Theory and Research of the International Federation of Library Associations and Institutions. The Round Table concentrates on universal and broad themes of library history, regional or international topics, and national or local experience of general significance. The website provides information on conferences, publications, and news of interest.

- Library History Round Table <http://www.spertus.edu/library-history/>

This is maintained by the Library History Round Table of the American Library Association. The Round Table aims to facilitate communication among students and scholars of Library History, and the website provides access to its newsletter, bibliographies, and other news of interest.

Index

A

Abbott Gerbert 86
Adams 154
Adelhard 31
Adelung 93
Aemilius Paulus 10
Aeneus Silvius Piccolomini 62
Agricola 63
Albareda, Mgr. Anselmo 115
Albert of Prussia 69
Albert V of Bavaria 70
Alcuin 25, 28, 32, 48
Alexander the Great 5, 7, 8
Althoff 105, 106, 112, 139
Ammianus Marcellinus 18
Amplonius of Erfurt 49
Anastasius 22
Apollo 13
Ariosto 59
Aristophanes 5
Aristophanes of Byzantium 7
Aristotle 5, 6, 43
Arno of Salzburg 33
Asinius Pollio 13

Assurbanipal 3, 4
Astor, John Jacob 120
Atticus 13
Audifreddi 85
August of Saxony 69
Augustine 43
Augustus 13
Augustus, Duke 76

B

Bacon 73, 83
Baluze 82, 85
Bandini 85
Barack 104
Barberini 115
Baronius 75
Beatus Rhenanus 65
Bede 24, 25
Bentley, Richard 84, 92
Benton Foundation 165
Bernward of Hildesheim 33
Biblioteca Benjamin Franklin 141
Bignon 82, 83
Billings, John Shaw 121

Bishop, William Warner 115
Blotius 70
Boccaccio 52
Bodley, Sir Thomas 73, 75, 84
Boineburg, von 90
Bojardo 100
Bonaparte, Jerome 97
Boniface VIII 44
Borghese 115
Borromeo, Federigo 75
Brant 65
Bray, Rev. Thomas 118, 124
Brühl, Count 92, 93, 94
Budd, John 165
Budé 60
Bugenhagen, John 68
Bünau, Count 92, 93
Burchard 33

C

Caesar 5, 7, 13, 76
Caesarius 23
Caliph Hakam II 42
Callimachus of Cyrene 7, 8
Cardinal Casanate 85
Cardinal d'Amboise 60, 72
Cardinal Mazarin 72, 73, 82
Carlo 75
Carnegie 115, 126, 140, 152
Carnegie, Andrew 122, 123, 125
Cassiodorus 22, 23, 25, 48, 65
Catherine II 89
Cavour 101
Cazden, Robert E. vii
Charlemagne 17, 23, 25, 28, 31, 32, 33
Charles Eugene of Württemberg 88
Charles IV 46, 48
Charles the Bald 25, 28
Charles the Bold 44
Charles V 43, 44
Charles VI 88
Charles VIII 60
Chaucer 60
Cicero 13, 14, 51
Clément 83, 90, 102
Cobbett 101

Cobham, Thomas 49
Cogswell, Joseph Green 120
Colbert 82, 90
Condé 67
Conrad III 31
Constantine 21
Coolidge 111
Coolidge Auditorium 154
Cotton, Robert 84
Cotton, Robert Bruce 84
Crerar Libraries 153

D

da Bisticci, Vespasiano 54, 55, 56
da Forli, Melozzo 59
Dalberg, von 63
Damasus 22
Dante 40
Davis, Donald G. 181
Davis, Jr., Donald G. 181
de Bury, Richard 40, 47, 49, 51
de Medici, Catherine 72
de Medici, Cosimo 52, 53, 54, 56
de Medici, Lorenzo 54
De Mendoza 71
de Pisan, Christine 43
de Romanis, Humbert 41
de Sorbonne, Robert 47
De Thou 73
de Tocqueville, Alexis 117
Delisle, Léopold 102, 103
Demetrius of Phalerum 7
dès Houssayes, Cotton 83
Descartes 73, 81
Desiderius 34
Dewey Decimal Classification 124, 131, 135, 140
Dewey, Melvil 121, 139
Diocletian 19
Downs, R.B. 138
Dubrovsky 89
Dury, John 84, 92
Dziatzko, Karl 112, 139

This book was set in Adobe Garamond type
by Michael Höhne
2001

Heritage Books by Don Heinrich Tolzmann:

Amana: William Rufus Perkins' and Barthinius L. Wick's
History of the Amana Society, or Community of True Inspiration

Americana Germanica: Paul Ben Baginsky's Bibliography of
German Works Relating to America, 1493–1800

Biography of Baron Von Steuben, the Army of the American Revolution and
Its Organizer: Rudolf Cronau's Biography of Baron von Steuben

CD: German-American Biographical Index (Midwest Families)

CD: Germans, Volume 2

CD: The German Colonial Era (four volumes)

Cincinnati's German Heritage

Covington's German Heritage

Custer: Frederick Whittaker's Complete Life of General George A. Custer,
Major General of Volunteers, Brevet Major General U.S. Army
and Lieutenant-Colonel Seventh U.S. Cavalry

Dayton's German Heritage: Karl Karstaedt's Golden Jubilee History of the
German Pioneer Society of Dayton, Ohio

Early German-American Newspapers: Daniel Miller's History

German Achievements in America: Rudolf Cronau's Survey History

German Americans in the Revolution

German Immigration to America: The First Wave

German Pioneer Life and Domestic Customs

German Pioneer Lifestyle

German Pioneers in Early California: Erwin G. Gudde's History

German-American Achievements: 400 Years of Contributions to America

German-Americana: A Bibliography

Germany and America, 1450–1700

Kentucky's German Pioneers: H. A. Rattermann's History

Lives and Exploits of the Daring Frank and Jesse James: Thaddeus Thorndike's
Graphic and Realistic Description of Their Many Deeds of Unparalleled
Daring in the Robbing of Banks and Railroad Trains

Louisiana's German Heritage: Louis Voss' Introductory History

Maryland's German Heritage: Daniel Wunderlich Nead's History

Memories of the Battle of New Ulm: Personal Accounts of the Sioux Uprising.
L. A. Fritsche's History of Brown County, Minnesota (1916)

Michigan's German Heritage: John Andrew Russell's History of the
German Influence in the Making of Michigan

Ohio's German Heritage

Outbreak and Massacre by the Dakota Indians in Minnesota in 1862: Marion P. Satterlee's
Minute Account of the Outbreak, with Exact Locations, Names of All Victims, Prisoners
at Camp Release, Refugees at Fort Ridgely, etc. Complete List of Indians Killed in

www.ingramcontent.com/pod-product-compliance
Lightning Source LLC
Chambersburg PA
CBHW081434270326
41932CB00019B/3204